The Flip Side II

60 More Point-of-View Monologs for Teens

HEAT

GAYLORD 5

Meriwether Publishing Ltd., Publisher
PO Box 7710
Colorado Springs, CO 80933-7710

Editor: Theodore O. Zapel
Typesetting: Sue Trinko
Cover design: Janice Melvin

Library of Congress Cataloging-in-Publication Data

Henderson, Heather H., 1970-
    The flip side II : 60 more point-of-view monologs for teens / by Heather H. Henderson.
    p. cm.
    Summary: A collection of monologues for contests and auditions, paired to present two different opinions on the same topic.
    ISBN 1-56608-074-6 (paper)
    1. Monologues. 2. Acting--Auditions. [1. Monologues. 2. Acting--Auditions.] I. Title: Flip side 2. II. Title.

PN2080.H44 2001
812'.54--dc21

        2001044909

1   2   3   4   01   02   03   04

For Michael
Who said I could, should and would
And gave up so much until I did

And for Coach Charlie Bynum —
World's Best Nag

Contents

Who We Are . . .

An Apple a Day

1   *(Actor breathes heavily into a paper bag. Breathes in and out*
2   *rapidly. After a pause ...)* **Nothing! Joey Lemanski said that this**
3   **would make me hyperventilate and puke.** *(Pause)* **Wait a**
4   **minute ... nope. Nothing.** *(Throws down paper bag and stomps*
5   *on it.)* **Man, this sucks. I must be the only kid on the planet who**
6   **can't get sick.**
7   **I know this kid in my History class that is absent at least**
8   **twice a week. Sometimes it's even as much as three days. He's**
9   **always sick. He sits in front of me and when he's not there, and**
10   **that's a lot, I always move up one seat. The days he is in school,**
11   **I'm not sure who is more surprised: the sick kid or the teacher.**
12   **She thinks his seat** *is* **my seat.**
13   **Me, on the other hand, I couldn't catch pneumonia if I**
14   **stood out in the freezing rain naked after visiting a TB ward.**
15   **My mom keeps telling me to be thankful that I've got my**
16   **health, that some kids aren't so fortunate, that I'll be glad**
17   **when I'm older. Who cares about when you're older? I need a**
18   **sick day now, not in fifty years! What's a kid got to do to miss**
19   **a day of school around here?**
20   **I'm not much of an actor, so the fake cough is out.**
21   *(Coughs.)* **See what I mean? Mom would be on to me like a**
22   **bum on a ham sandwich.** *(Heavy sigh)* **There's no hope. I'll just**
23   **have to suck it up and face Leah in school on Monday. Damn.**
24   **I'll be the laughing stock of the whole eighth grade.**
25   **See, Leah is this fabulous girl. She's got dark brown hair**
26   **and a perfect smile. Her eyes are so dark that you think there's**
27   **been an eclipse. And so popular that she's way out of my**
28   **league. I mean, face it. We all know what category we're in,**
29   **don't we? I've been penciled in as the geeky, straight A nerd**
30   **since I won the perfect attendance award in Ms. Nippins' class**

1   in the fourth grade. Heck, you'd get straight A's too if you
2   had to sit in class all day everyday.
3   Anyway, Leah's at her locker collecting her books at the
4   end of the day. I'm taking my time putting my books away
5   just for the chance to look at her. All of a sudden, she flashes
6   me this dazzling smile. I smile back, but I'm thinking, me?
7   So, I point to myself and and mouth the word, me. She
8   puckers up and pretends to blow me a kiss. At this point,
9   I'm dying. I'm telling you, this girl is the next Miss
10 America. I slam my locker shut and start to walk in her
11 direction when this huge mountain of a kid strolls past me,
12 walks right up to Leah, and gets lip-locked with her right
13 there in the hallway. He was halfway down her throat, and
14 all I could think was "stupid, stupid, stupid." Gary Olsen,
15 the mountain of a kid, has the locker directly behind mine.
16 She wasn't blowing kisses at me. She was blowing kisses at
17 him!
18   I tried to make it look as though I was going up to talk
19 to her on purpose since I was already walking in her
20 direction. They're going at it and I'm just standing there
21 'cause I don't know what else to do. Gary gets the feeling
22 that they're no longer alone and lets go. Then we all stare at
23 each other.
24   "Um, I was absent yesterday. Do you have the
25 homework from algebra?" I don't know what I was
26 thinking. I choked.
27   "Aren't you that kid who's never been absent," she
28 asks. Apparently, this much schooling has made me more
29 stupid instead of smarter. I wanted to vanish. I can't show
30 my face in that hallway again.
31   So, anyone here with tonsillitis? A nice-phlegm wracked
32 cough? I'd like to take you out to share a one-straw soda.
33 Come on. Do a guy a favor. Infect me! Please?
34
35

Great Green Globs of Greasy Grimy Gopher Guts

1   **Dob anydoby hab un tisew?** *(Looks helplessly to the*
2   *audience for a tissue.)* **Anydoby?** *(Frantically searches pockets.*
3   *Checks shirtsleeves. Finds a tissue up one shirtsleeve. Sighs with*
4   *exaggerated relief. Uncrumples the tissue and blows nose loudly.)*
5   **Ah, that's better.**
6   **I'm always sick. You can ask anybody. I've missed forty-**
7   **one school days this year, and I've got the doctor's notes to**
8   **prove it. Some kids are lucky enough to be able to fake an**
9   **illness or develop a phony fever. They get to stay home,**
10   **enjoying their time while they waste the afternoon away. Me?**
11   **I'd give anything to spend the day at school! I'm so sick so**
12   **often that a day of geography and English grammar lectures**
13   **sounds like pure heaven. Now that's sick!**
14   **I've always been sickly. When I was born, premature, of**
15   **course, I had jaundice. That's where you turn a funny yellow**
16   **color 'cause something's not right with your liver. After the**
17   **jaundice, I got colic. Colic is like bad gas. Then it was an**
18   **allergy to milk.**
19   **Speaking of allergies, I'm allergic to practically**
20   **everything. Come on. Name something.** *(Wait for audience*
21   *response.)* **Yup, that.** *(Audience response)* **That too.** *(Audience*
22   *response)* **Oh, definitely. In the summer, I'm allergic to fresh**
23   **cut grass. In the winter, it's wood smoke. I'm allergic to**
24   **chocolate so there goes any hope of a decent Halloween or**
25   **Easter. I wheeze when I run. I wheeze when I laugh too hard.**
26   **The only safe pet for me is a goldfish, but even then, I have to**
27   **wash my hands immediately after feeding Goldy 'cause if I**
28   **don't, I get red, splotchy hives from touching the food. Excuse**
29   **me.** *(Blows nose again. Hacking cough)*
30   **In the first grade, I got chicken pox. In the second, it was**

1 bronchitis. The bronchitis turned into double pneumonia. I
2 almost died. Really. In the third grade, I got ... *(Looks*
3 *around and whispers)* ... lice. It's not really a disease, but I
4 did catch it from Susie Sherman. *(Shudders at the thought.)*
5 Things went relatively well in fourth and fifth grade. I had
6 my allergies to deal with, but then I always do. Sixth grade
7 was a banner year. I'm lucky that I was there to have my
8 picture taken for the yearbook, otherwise the kids wouldn't
9 have known who I was. Appendicitis, tonsillitis, broke my
10 foot and then my arm. Got braces and glasses. Some kids
11 have nicknames, like Spud, or Fast Eddy. That year I was
12 known as the "Sick Kid."
13   Basically, I'm a lemon. If I were a car, my parents would
14 have traded me in by now. *(Wipes nose on sleeve. Sniffs*
15 *loudly.)* Unbelievably, I feel pretty good this year. I go to
16 school on most days. My mom packs me a gluten-free,
17 wheat-free, milk-free lunch. I pack my tissues and inhaler,
18 take my multi-vitamin and go. Except for PE, I'm like a
19 normal kid. Well, almost normal, especially when you've
20 been known as the "Sick Kid."
21
22
23
24
25
26
27
28
29
30
31
32
33
34
35

Country Boy

1   Will ya take a look at that? *(Gazes out over the heads of the*
2   *audience.)* **Gosh, that there is one of the purtiest darn sunsets**
3   **that I ever laid eyes on. I ain't been too long on this here**
4   **planet, but I know God's handiwork when I see it. The whole**
5   **darn hillside is painted in gold.** *(Long whistle)* **Hills is gold,**
6   **trees is gold, even the sky is kinda like a bluish gold. Yup,**
7   **couldn't pay me 'nuf to trade all this fer some grimy, gritty**
8   **city. I've been a country boy all my life and I'll go to my grave**
9   **the same. Granddaddy says you can take the boy out of the**
10   **country but you can't take the country out of the boy. True**
11   **enough. But this is one country boy who ain't even gonna risk**
12   **it to find out.**
13   **It ain't like I never been somewheres else. I been to the city**
14   **a few times. Don't see what the big deal is all about. There are**
15   **so many people and buildings and noise all piled up so close**
16   **together, well, a body can't even think a thought. The air is so**
17   **thick and gritty you can taste it, and believe me, it's worse**
18   **than pig slop. Them fancy neon signs light up the sky so you**
19   **can't even see the moon, let alone the stars.**
20   **And the city is downright costly, too. Why, a steak is**
21   **$22.50! $22.50! And it weren't even a good piece of meat**
22   **neither. What I like least about the city is the meanness. People**
23   **feel mean, look mean and act mean in the city. One time I see**
24   **this fella all dressed up in some fancy suit jump into a taxicab**
25   **that had stopped to pick up a young mother and her baby girl.**
26   **Just pushed her out of the way and got in. Didn't look back or**
27   **nothing. My daddy and I got real angry about it. We waited**
28   **with that lady until the next cab stopped for her and then**
29   **guarded the doors so no more fancy men in Sunday suits could**
30   **snatch that cab out from under her. She must've said thank**

1   you a thousand times or more. Wasn't nothing. Just
2   niceness. Seems the city'd be almost bearable if there was a
3   little more niceness.
4   Out here, we gotta be nice if we're gonna make it. When
5   Daddy's tractor broke just before the harvest, folks liked to
6   lend a hand. By nightfall, Daddy had his pick of five
7   different tractors from our neighbors. Then there was the
8   year of the flood. Folks from all over pitched in to help each
9   other out. I was real little but I still remember bringing old
10   Mrs. White the pillow off my bed 'cause I heard she had no
11   bed at all! Everyone thought it was real cute, but I was
12   deadly serious. If you ain't got a bed, you need a pillow!
13   Yup, I'd rather be nice and live in the country than be
14   an ole meany up there in the city. The air here smells like
15   berries. There's plenty of space, and the only blinking lights
16   are the fireflies in the meadow.
17   *(Looks back out over the heads of the audience.)* **Sure was**
18   **a pretty sunset.**
19
20
21
22
23
24
25
26
27
28
29
30
31
32
33
34
35

City Slicker

1   *(To imaginary character)* **Yes, go down to the end of the**
2   **block, turn right and continue north three blocks. Take the**
3   **subway to the Center Street stop. You'll see the signs in the**
4   **station pointing you in the right direction.** *(Pause)* **On second**
5   **thought. Let me call you a cab.** *(Whistles.)* **Taxi!** *(Pause)* **You're**
6   **welcome.** *(Disgusted)* **Tourists. I love when they decide** *(Affects*
7   *an exagerated country accent)* **to hitch up the buggy and go into**
8   **town!** *(Looks Off-stage and slowly shakes head.)* **They'd be lost**
9   **before they crossed the street.**

10   **My uncle taught me how to call a cab when I was eight. A**
11   **taxi won't even notice you at rush hour if you don't whistle.**
12   **See, I had dance class uptown and Mom didn't want me to**
13   **take the subway all by myself. So, I perfected the whistle. In**
14   **this city, it's survival of the fittest. Since I'm still here, I must**
15   **be doing OK.**

16   **I've lived in the city all my life. Not that I was born**
17   **here — actually, I came from some little hick town called**
18   **Pleasant Junction — but I've lived here long enough to fool**
19   **the natives. I suppose if we'd stayed in Pleasant Junction I'd**
20   **have turned out differently. I'd probably be something boring**
21   **— one of those shy, quiet types. But the city doesn't do shy and**
22   **quiet. You gotta be tough to live here. If you're part of the city,**
23   **you walk fast, talk fast, think fast. The beat of the city keeps**
24   **you moving. It's like a waterfall. Once you get caught up in the**
25   **current, you gotta keep moving until over you go. Can you feel**
26   **it? Every city has its own beat; you've just got to stop long**
27   **enough to feel it. That's about the only time I slow down.**
28   **There's so much to see and do.**

29   **I can go to a movie, a concert, a play, pick a sporting event.**
30   **I can visit a museum or go to the zoo. Shop, eat, dance. The**

1   city just keeps me go, go, going. That's why these country
2   types flounder along. They try to slow down. They struggle
3   against the current, trying to keep their heads up. Go with
4   the flow. That's what my uncle always says.
5   Now there is one group that doesn't move with the beat
6   of the city. In fact, Cora and her friends each kinda move to
7   their own beat. Everyday on my way to P.S. 168 (that stands
8   for public school if you didn't know, country boy) I stop to
9   give Cora some of my lunch money. She lives in the
10   doorway outside of Mr. Kim's Takee Outee Chinese
11   Restaurant. Cora used to move fast, but when her husband
12   and daughter died, she decided to slow down permanently
13   so she wouldn't miss any more stuff. She asks me about
14   school and my friends. She's nice, even if she hasn't always
15   got it together up here. *(Points to head.)*
16   Well, I've slowed down long enough. I'm late for the
17   Screaming Meanies concert downtown. Taxi! Taxi!
18   *(Whistles.)* **Taxi!** *(Runs Off-stage.)*
19
20
21
22
23
24
25
26
27
28
29
30
31
32
33
34
35

Outside? Ick!

1   The greatest invention ever created on this planet was
2 climate control. As far as I'm concerned, they could just pave
3 over every forest, fill every valley and drain every pond. Do
4 away with the outdoors altogether! Either that or create a big
5 bubble over towns and parks and stuff so you could air-
6 condition the place to the desired temperature and remain
7 cool and comfy all year long.
8   The ideal environment is the mall. Need food? Go to the
9 snack court. Tired? Find the beds in a major department
10 store. Clothing? Music? Entertainment? Done. Movie
11 theaters, skating rinks, you name it. All under one perfectly
12 temperate, bug and ultra-violet free roof. Why bother with the
13 real thing when you have perfectly manicured trees and
14 shrubbery, birds and fountains. Throw in a few seasonal
15 flowers and you're looking at a virtual Garden of Eden.
16   Last summer, my parents thought it would be a good idea
17 to "get back to nature." They rented a cabin in the mountains
18 way out in the middle of nowhere. It was three rooms. That's
19 it! A living area, a big bedroom (with no bed, might I add) and
20 a bathroom. Thank God, it had a working toilet or I might
21 have hitchhiked out of there that instant. We had to sleep on
22 the floor in sleeping bags, cook our food outside in a cooking
23 pit and suffer enough family bonding to last a lifetime. By the
24 end of the week, my back hurt from sleeping on the floor, I had
25 enough bug bites to rival a case of chicken pox and my hair
26 was so greasy that I considered shaving my head. We took cold
27 showers, ate cold food and froze all night long.
28   Mom was so sick of trying to cook in that fire pit that she
29 finally refused to cook another meal. To keep from starving,
30 we piled in the car and drove eleven and a half miles down

1 winding roads to some crappy little town to eat bad food
2 from a diner. Best meal I ever had in my whole life!
3   By the time we got home, I hated my family, I hated
4 vacations and I especially hated nature. I made a solemn
5 vow that I would never again set foot outside unless my life
6 depended on it.
7   Dad's hinting at another nature-lover's vacation again
8 this year. Something about driving out West to see the
9 Grand Canyon before it's gone. It's several million years
10 old. Where's it going? Anyway, I've already said that the
11 only way I'll go is if, at the end of the day, there's a hot
12 shower in a cool hotel room with a soft bed and room
13 service at the touch of a button. Man evolved to be more
14 comfortable. Nature is for the birds.
15
16
17
18
19
20
21
22
23
24
25
26
27
28
29
30
31
32
33
34
35

Nature Lover

1   Can you smell it? *(Deep sniff)* Doesn't the salt air just make
2 you feel alive? I'll never understand how those "indoor" types
3 do it. I mean, who could stay inside on a day like this?
4   I've always been the outdoorsy type. It's mostly my
5 parent's fault. They're nature lovers too. Ever since I could
6 first toddle, I've toddled straight out of the door. It's like
7 nature was calling to me. Mom says it didn't matter what
8 season it was, whenever it was time to go in, I'd throw a
9 temper tantrum. Kicking and screaming, arms pounding, the
10 works. Who could blame me? What toy could ever compare to
11 the beach with its miles of sand, endless waves to ride, people
12 to watch? My favorite thing to do on a hot day was to bury
13 myself deep in the sand. At first, the sand was cool, and it felt
14 like the beach was giving me a hug. After I'd baked good and
15 long in the sun, I'd tumble out and run for the water looking
16 like some powdered donut. Aah ... one splash and I was cool
17 and clean all over again.
18   The beach is undoubtedly my favorite place but it really
19 doesn't matter as long as it's outside. I love the mountains;
20 they make me feel so small. I love the bigness of an open
21 prairie. The sky looks as if it could just swallow me up and I'm
22 afraid to speak because my voice doesn't begin to fill the
23 space. I love the snow and ice, tornadoes and hurricanes,
24 spring, summer and fall. The crunch of the dry leaves, the
25 crunch of cracking ice. Everything!
26   My parents encourage me too. We've gone camping every
27 Memorial Day that I can remember. Last year when I turned
28 thirteen, Dad and I started hiking the Appalachian Trail. It
29 was in honor of the start of my teenage years. Yup, we plan to
30 hike all two thousand, one hundred, sixty-seven miles of it

1   before I turn twenty. That's our goal anyway. It was hard at
2   first 'cause you've really got to push yourself. You can't just
3   wander from place to place — you really have got to move.
4   But at night, when we'd stop to make camp, the sun would
5   dip down and peek between the trees as if to say good night.
6   The fireflies would appear and the night noises would start.
7   We'd light a small campfire to cook our food and then we'd
8   sit and listen. If you're really quiet, you can hear the woods
9   come alive. Crickets, owls, mice and raccoons. Even
10   bobcats. It's not scary like all those indoor types think it
11   would be. It's … amazing. Anyway, that's our plan. Our
12   annual trip is still a long time away. I'm really looking
13   forward to it. But right now, I'm gonna dig a deep hole,
14   bury myself deep in the sand and listen to the surf roll in.
15   Care to join me?
16
17
18
19
20
21
22
23
24
25
26
27
28
29
30
31
32
33
34
35

Candies and Cookies and Cakes ... Oh My!

1   Excuse me while I finish this. *(Continues chewing, licks*
2 *fingers and smacks lips. Burps loudly.)* **Sorry. Better out than in.**
3 **I'll be the first to admit I'm addicted to this stuff.** *(Holds up the*
4 *bag.)* **Both my doctor and my mother worry about my eating**
5 **habits, but it's not like I'm fat or anorexic or something. I just**
6 **know what I like.**
7   **It's not that my parents haven't tried. My friends still**
8 **tease me about the beef tongue meatloaf, mashed parsnips and**
9 **steamed cauliflower my mom served us at my slumber party.**
10 **"Mom," I asked. "This is party food?" Do you know what she**
11 **said? "You'll thank me when you're my age." Like anyone**
12 **could live to my mom's age eating that crap. Why, that's the**
13 **stuff that'll kill you! Health food companies start rumors that**
14 **junk food is bad to boost their sales but the truth is eating junk**
15 **food only makes you live longer. The preservatives that keep**
16 **the food fresh will do the same to you if you eat enough. At the**
17 **rate I'm going, I'll live to two hundred seventy!**
18   **In the morning, I have a can of Pepsi and a package of**
19 **chocolate Pop Tarts — the kind with the sprinkles. Usually, I**
20 **bring along a mini-box of Fruit Loops just in case I'm still**
21 **hungry. The truth is, most of the time, I just eat them because**
22 **the box is so cute. For lunch, it's two bags of barbecue potato**
23 **chips and one bag of sour cream and ranch style. I wash them**
24 **down with another Pepsi and a Twinkie. If I'm desperate, I'll**
25 **have a piece of pizza from the cafeteria, but not often. Come**
26 **on. School lunches? That stuff will kill you! When school's**
27 **over, I'll have a Popsicle or some ice cream to take me over**
28 **until dinner. Mom and Dad usually have something so gross**
29 **that I make my own. Most of the time, it's hot dogs or mac and**
30 **cheese from the box. I like nachos with lots of cheese dip. Not**

1 real cheese, of course. Spray cheese out of the can. Stick it
2 in the microwave for two minutes and *voila*! Dinner is
3 served.
4   I'm not sure how it started. I used to like grapes and
5 berries and stuff. Now I wouldn't eat a grape if you paid me
6 and the only berries I eat are in pie. Vegetables are totally
7 out unless they're deep-fried and slathered in ketchup.
8 Hamburgers are about the only meat I'll eat. That and
9 hotdogs. Chicken is gross. Pork is worse and don't even get
10 me started on something exotic like veal or lamb. Poor baby
11 animals. And you think what I eat is gross! Fish sticks are
12 OK, but offer me some big, slimy pop-eyed fish in a deli case
13 and I'll turn green faster than spoiled meat.
14   I'll admit. This diet isn't for everyone. It takes a strong
15 stomach to endure deep fried, multi-processed, vitamin-less
16 foods, but faced with the choice of stir-fried octopus or a
17 can of Spaghetti-Os, hand me the can opener any day. Bon
18 appetit!
19
20
21
22
23
24
25
26
27
28
29
30
31
32
33
34
35

Health Nut

1   *(Student jogs On-stage. When Center Stage, begins jumping*
2   *jacks. Mid-set, switch to stretches. Throughout monolog, continue*
3   *stretching, leg lifts, pump arms, etc.)* ... **five, six, seven. Excuse**
4   **me while I finish this set ... eight, nine, ten. I didn't always act**
5   **like this. I used to be a great big, fat couch potato. After my**
6   **parents got divorced, I ate whenever I felt sad, which was all**
7   **the time. Bags of chips, chocolate ice cream, you name it. And**
8   **mountains of it. By the time I hit middle school, I weighed one**
9   **hundred sixty. Considering that I'm only five feet tall, I was**
10 **way over my ideal weight limit. Since we all had to take**
11 **elective classes, I chose dance. My doctor said absolutely not!**
12 **He thought that exercise would be good for me, but I just**
13 **couldn't jump right in. I'd have to lose some weight before**
14 **he'd allow it. Guess what I got stuck with instead? Home Ec.**
15 **At first, I was really mad. It wasn't fair. Bye ice cream. Bye**
16 **chips. Bye cookies. It was an apple a day and join a health club**
17 **or else. The surprising thing was that I actually liked it. I**
18 **didn't mind the exercise. Sweating wasn't a big deal after all.**
19 **I looked forward to aerobics and weight training. Once I**
20 **started to exercise, suddenly, food wasn't a big deal either.**
21 **Home Ec helped me to see that a body does better on the food**
22 **pyramid than a Death By Chocolate. I started to see food as**
23 **fuel, like a car. The better the quality, the better I worked out.**
24 **Soon, I was down to a hundred and five and benching almost**
25 **the same. Now I can't seem to stop. If I do twenty push-ups**
26 **one day, I have to do twenty-five the next. If I run three miles,**
27 **then I run three and a quarter. Everyday I push myself a little**
28 **harder, a little stronger and a little faster.**
29   **Now, when I look at old pictures of myself, I can't believe**
30 **who I was. I'm not sure I could go back to couch potato if I**

1 wanted to. Even my parents are slimming down and lifting
2 weights. Separately, but my attitude has rubbed off on both
3 of them. A healthful lifestyle is my way of life. Besides, I've
4 made the dance team for the second year in a row. I'm not
5 willing to start sitting in the wings now.
6
7
8
9
10
11
12
13
14
15
16
17
18
19
20
21
22
23
24
25
26
27
28
29
30
31
32
33
34
35

Domestic God

1   Some people would never admit this, but I clean one mean
2 toilet. Yup, there's nothing like looking down at a sparkling,
3 freshly sanitized bowl to make you feel proud. C'mon. Admit
4 it. Don't you check out how grungy someone's toilet is before
5 you sit down? In public places, you can tell which
6 establishments employ a janitorial staff that feels pride in
7 their work. At least I can. See, when my dad left us, Mom had
8 to go back to work full-time. With no one else at home, guess
9 who inherited the housework?

10   At first, I hated it. I mean, what kid ever volunteers to
11 clean their room, let alone like the job? But the more I did it,
12 the better I got. It was kinda like a contest with myself. How
13 tightly could I make the bed? How many different meals could
14 I make from hamburger? How quickly could I clean the
15 bathroom tub? It used to take me forever, but now I'm down
16 to a speedy three minutes, thirty-six seconds. I figured out that
17 if you have a schedule, the whole cleaning job is easier. Then
18 once stuff is already clean, it's easier to keep clean. It gets me
19 a faster time too. So, I run a tight ship. No shoes in the house.
20 All laundry has to be turned right side out before it hits the
21 wash, and absolutely no eating in the living room. My friends
22 tease me, but most of their moms pick up after them. I'm the
23 one cleaning up, so I make the rules!

24   Now, when I read, it's *Good Housekeeping* instead of
25 *Godzilla*. It's a one-stop kind of magazine: home decorating,
26 tasty recipes, cleaning tips. It's got it all. I'm also strangely
27 attracted to cleaning gadgets. Last Christmas, I actually asked
28 Mom for a dust mop. A dust mop? At my age? Really. It was
29 starting to bug me that the dust kept accumulating under the
30 bedroom dresser. Mom thought a dust mop was an odd

1   request too. But I don't often see her complaining when she
2   comes home to freshly mopped floors, clean laundry and
3   my newest hamburger casserole creation. Yes, someday, I'm
4   gonna make some woman very happy. I'm the perfect
5   catch. A regular domestic god.
6
7
8
9
10
11
12
13
14
15
16
17
18
19
20
21
22
23
24
25
26
27
28
29
30
31
32
33
34
35

Handy (Wo)man

1   My daddy said I was born with a hammer in one hand and
2   a fistful of nails in the other. That I reached down to cut my
3   own umbilical cord, and then proceeded to renovate the
4   hospital wing. He's kidding, of course, but it does seem like
5   I've always been handy with tools. When I was four, I could
6   build a birdhouse. A really simple one, but hey, I'm talking
7   four years old! By the time I was ten, I was regularly working
8   with Dad on construction jobs. See, Dad's a carpenter, and
9   builds houses and other stuff for people. I used to sink
10   finishing nails and then fill them with wood filler. That's the
11   putty stuff like Play-Doh that you put in holes so you don't see
12   where the nail went in when you paint. I'd get two cents a nail.
13   Considering that a carpenter can use a thousand nails on a
14   job, I made a bundle. I'd also collect wood scraps for my own
15   projects. I've made boxes, key ring holders, picture frames,
16   you name it. I can measure, saw or miter with the best of them.
17   This year when I turned thirteen, Dad got me a power
18   drill. He figured that since I was growing up, I could handle it.
19   Boy, was I ready for power tools. Try putting together a
20   bookcase or a bike with a regular screwdriver, and you'll see
21   what I mean. His friends teased him a lot. "A power drill? For
22   a girl?" Like the only things girls should play with are dolls
23   and clothes and stuff. But Dad just shrugged it off and got it
24   for me anyway. It's a whole lot more fun than a boring doll.
25   When Mom died, Dad couldn't afford daycare, so he
26   brought me to his jobs. People used to look at him funny
27   coming to a construction site with a toddler, but there was no
28   other way. I had my own little hardhat and work boots. Dad
29   would tie a piece of rope to the back of my overalls so I
30   couldn't wander off. I would play with the wood scraps like

1   blocks. Dad gave me my own little hammer, and I'd bang on
2   stuff just like him. The sound of the buzz saw put me to
3   sleep at naptime. Like I said, by the time I was ten, I was an
4   old hand at construction. I was sad when I started school.
5   I'll admit it; I love demolition. It's a great way to take
6   out the frustrations of the day. But I love construction more.
7   I'm really good at it. I measure twice and cut once (that's a
8   rule you never break). It feels so good to sit on or open or
9   hang something up on a piece of furniture you've made.
10   Right now, Dad and I are framing a window seat for my
11   room. It has two bookcases on both sides and a lift-top
12   storage bench for seating. It even has a drawer in it. It's my
13   most complicated project yet, but I'm ready. After all, I was
14   born with a hammer in one hand and a fist full of nails in
15   the other.
16
17
18
19
20
21
22
23
24
25
26
27
28
29
30
31
32
33
34
35

Early Bird

1   Did I wake you? I was just coming back in from watching
2   the sunrise. I love to see the beginning of a new day. First, the
3   darkness turns all gray. Then, the tiniest sliver of pale light
4   throws color into all that grayness. The clouds turn pink. The
5   birds start chirping and before you know it, the sun is up and
6   the day is here. No matter how many times I've seen the
7   sunrise, it's like magic.

8   I've always been an early bird. When I was little, my mom
9   used to try to convince me that I needed to go back to sleep,
10   but I think she was the one who really needed the rest. It
11   wasn't long before she stopped trying and stayed in bed. Now,
12   I get up as early as I want to.

13   It's as if I have an alarm clock inside of me. I wake up
14   around five a.m. everyday. Most people who aren't early birds
15   would think it was still nighttime, but us early birds know
16   the difference. The morning feels ... fresh. Like a possibility.
17   Anything could happen, and I get to see it all.

18   That's definitely the best part of being an early bird. Lots
19   of people complain that there aren't enough hours in the day.
20   Not for me. I have all the time I need.

21   I wake up and watch the sunrise. I hardly ever miss it.
22   Then I go for a walk. I like to see the world come alive. People
23   will walk outside in their pajamas; something they wouldn't
24   be caught dead doing at noon. They move in slow motion. The
25   breeze is gentle. The light is soft. The whole world moves at a
26   different pace. As the sun rises, the pace picks up. By the time
27   I finish my walk, I've still got plenty of time to eat breakfast,
28   get dressed and do my homework before school. After school,
29   I have lots of free time that other kids don't have, 'cause I
30   don't use up my afternoons doing homework.

1   The only bad thing about being an early bird is that by
2   four o'clock, I'm pooped. I can barely keep my eyes open
3   during dinner, so on most nights, I'm in bed by eight thirty.
4   Lots of my friends stay up until ten or later. I've tried, but
5   I never make it. Besides, who wants to sit around and look
6   at the dark? You can't see anything! I'd rather spend my
7   nighttime sleeping. Before you know it, the light will come
8   sneaking across the grass and start tapping on my window.
9   The birds will be chirping a morning hello and the world
10   will slowly come alive again. I'd rather be awake to see the
11   magic.
12
13
14
15
16
17
18
19
20
21
22
23
24
25
26
27
28
29
30
31
32
33
34
35

Night Owl

1   Oh, I'm sorry. Did I wake you? I was just coming down for
2   a snack. There's something about having a bowl of cereal or
3   the last brownie at midnight that makes them taste better.
4   Mom and Dad know I'm a night owl, so they're not
5   surprised when they find dishes in the sink the next morning.
6   The only time Mom had a fit was when I left a half gallon of
7   Rocky Road ice cream on the counter ... all night long. Once
8   it melted, it leaked through the carton, onto the counter and
9   dribbled onto the floor. When Mom came down the next
10   morning, she found me asleep at the table, and a steady parade
11   of ants crawling in and out of the ice cream. Let's just say she
12   was a little ticked off.
13   Usually I don't fall asleep at the table, but that was a very
14   late night. I didn't head down for a snack until three thirty in
15   the morning. I couldn't put down the latest installment in *The*
16   *Wizard Chronicles.* By the time I finally closed the cover, it was
17   past snack time. The hardest part was getting up for school at
18   six thirty. Even if I stay up all night long, Mom and Dad insist
19   that I go to school the next day. If I'm so much as tardy to
20   homeroom, then I have a bedtime for a month. Not that I'll fall
21   asleep, but a bedtime in this house means, no lights, no books,
22   no TV, no radio. Just bed and nothing else. So, the idea of
23   staring into the darkness for hours on end is enough
24   motivation to get me up on even the hardest mornings.
25   Most of the time, I spend my nights reading. I'm a chronic
26   reader. If I start a book, no matter how long it is, I have to
27   finish it before I can go to sleep. One more chapter isn't
28   enough for me. I have to read them all. I have to know what
29   happens.
30   But it's the same with TV shows. If I start watching a

1 show, even two or three minutes worth, then I might as well
2 settle in for the long haul 'cause I'll end up watching the
3 whole thing. Same for CDs, computer games, anything. I
4 have to finish them. So usually it's after midnight before I
5 turn out the light.
6   Since I can't start any project until after all my
7 homework is done (and that's always after dinner), the only
8 time I have to myself is late at night. But it is more than
9 that. I like the darkness, the quiet. I like the long gray
10 shadows and the moonlight. No one bothers you because
11 they're all asleep. It's very peaceful.
12   I think I was an owl in another life. When I'm older, I'll
13 definitely find a job that has a night shift. That way, I can
14 sleep during the day, and not waste one second of the night.
15 Given the choice between an owl and an early bird, I'd
16 definitely choose to be an owl. The early bird may get the
17 worm, but night owls get the last brownie.
18
19
20
21
22
23
24
25
26
27
28
29
30
31
32
33
34
35

I Gotta Be Me!

1   There are days when I'd sell my soul to trade in my face.
2   Everyone thinks that being a twin must be the neatest
3   biological phenomenon that could ever happen to anyone, but
4   really, there's nothing neat about it. On most days, it's just a
5   big pain in the butt.
6   Take today, for instance. My alarm goes off. I get up, get
7   showered and get dressed. I'm feeling relatively happy for a
8   school day. I'm two steps out of my bedroom door when my
9   older sister, Kristin, starts screaming from across the hall
10   about how I'd better return her green sweater 'cause she's got
11   a date tonight and it'd better not be ripped like last time, and
12   blah, blah, blah. I'm clueless. She's freaking out at the top of
13   her lungs, and I have no idea what she's yelling about. All of a
14   sudden, this green sweater comes flying past my head and
15   lands at Kristin's feet. My twin sister, Krissy, yells, "Take it!"
16   and slams our bedroom door. I'm standing there dazed.
17   "Sorry, Kate," Kristin says. "I thought you were Krissy." Most
18   people check to make sure they've got the right person before
19   they start accusing them of stealing. If you're a twin, you're
20   responsible for your sister's crimes as well.
21   After I got off the school bus, this guy Bobby, who is so hot
22   I could melt just being in his presence, comes up to me. I smile
23   and try to act real cool, but the whole time my insides are all
24   loopy because his sparkly, blue eyes are looking at *me*. "Are
25   you Kate or Krissy?" he says. "I'm Kate," I say and I try to
26   make my voice sound all soft and sexy. "Good," he said.
27   "Could you give this note to Krissy? Man, that girl is a babe!"
28   A babe? If we look so much alike that he couldn't tell us apart
29   a minute ago, then why is she a babe and I'm not? If I could
30   throw better I would've beamed him in the head with that

1   note.
2   The day just got worse from there. In biology class, our
3   teacher, Mr. Eastman, made me and Krissy stand up in
4   front of the room while he pointed out our differences. It
5   was kind of nice to have someone explain that we aren't the
6   same, but I felt like part of a sideshow. There's Mr. Eastman
7   explaining all about genes and chromosomes and I'm
8   standing there feeling like an idiot. With other kids, it's
9   obvious that they don't look alike. I hate having to look like
10 a dork before other people realize I'm different too.
11   During lunch, Krissy's friend, Jackie, who isn't known
12 for her staggering intellect, asked us the most stupid
13 question on the planet. "How do you know you're you
14 and not the other person?" Fortunately, Krissy handled it.
15 "Because we're different people, you moron! We just look
16 alike." Personally, I think Jackie was more confused than
17 ever.
18   But that's the hardest part of being a twin. People
19 expect you to be like someone else just because you look like
20 them. Krissy and I may be mirror images of each other but
21 that's where the resemblance stops. We're so different but
22 nobody seems to notice. If you can't judge a book by its
23 cover, then why do it with people? I'm telling you, some
24 days I'd sell my soul to trade in my face. At least then, I'd
25 have something of my own.
26
27
28
29
30
31
32
33
34
35

Mirror Image

1 There are days when it pays to be a twin! Sure, some days
2 are tough, but then there are the days like today that make it
3 all worth it.
4   See, there's this guy Bobby, who my sister Kate thinks is
5 God's gift to women everywhere. He's all right I guess, but
6 he's such a nerd I can hardly stand to have him in my personal
7 space. He sits really close to me, trying to help me with my
8 math, when all I'm doing is copying off his papers. I think he
9 knows this but he doesn't care just as long as he can sit next to
10 me. What a dork!
11   Anyway, yesterday, after we got home, Kate just about
12 pokes my eye out with this paper airplane note she's flown at
13 me from across our room. I ask her all nice who's it from, and
14 she gives me this huge attitude that she doesn't know and
15 doesn't care. Well, duh, she obviously must know 'cause she's
16 passing it on from the owner. Sometimes, she's a real pain in
17 the butt.
18   So, the note's from Bobby who wants me to meet him at
19 the skating rink after school on Friday. The skating rink? I
20 stopped going there in the sixth grade. Only geeks and dorks
21 hang out at the skating rink anymore. I wouldn't be caught
22 dead at the skating rink. But, I've got a huge math test coming
23 up soon, so I can't totally blow off Bobby. All this time, Kate is
24 acting like she's doing homework, but I know she's not 'cause
25 she's turning the pages so hard that I'm betting she'll rip one
26 any minute. Then I get this brilliant idea. A truly stunning idea
27 that will only work if you're a twin. I'm a genius.
28   "Katie," I said. "Would you please go to the skating rink
29 on Friday and pretend to be me?" At first, she refuses, but I
30 make a big deal out of begging her to take my place with

1   Bobby. I could see her biting her lip 'cause she was trying
2   not to say yes so I really turned on the charm. If Kate likes
3   Bobby, and Bobby likes me, and I don't want to be seen at
4   the skating rink, and Katie and I look so much alike that
5   even Mom has trouble telling us apart whenever we're
6   rushing around, then who's it gonna hurt if we switch
7   places? What good is being a twin if you can't make it work
8   for you?

9   Kate decides that she'll go if I make her bed every
10   morning for a week and empty the dishwasher the night it's
11   her turn, but she only said that so it'd look like she didn't
12   care. If you ask me, she'd have done it for free, but she had
13   to make it look like she could take Bobby or leave Bobby
14   since he made her deliver his mail.

15   So today, I dressed her up in my clothes and for once,
16   she really looked good. Mom took Kate and her friend,
17   Colleen, to the skating rink and I was off the hook! 'Course
18   I was dying to know what she was doing and saying as me.
19   I'd have to beat on her a little if she screwed up my
20   reputation. But I didn't care just as long as I didn't have to
21   be seen with Bobby outside of school.

22   Hours and hours later, Kate came home and she was all
23   smiley and was positively dying to know what happened. I
24   didn't even pretend not to care; I just busted out with all
25   the questions I'd thought of since she'd left and made her
26   tell me everything. I guess they talked about all kinds of
27   books and weird English movies and the environment or
28   something and Bobby was so impressed with me (really
29   Kate) that he kissed her after one of those couple skates.
30   Kate was so excited about kissing Bobby that she told him
31   she was Kate and not me, and guess what? He had such a
32   great time that he didn't care! Can you believe it? He'd just
33   been the victim of a great twin joke and he didn't care,
34   because my sister thinks that it's vitally important to cut the
35   plastic rings on soda cans! To top it all off, Bobby even

1 agreed to keep helping me with my math as some personal
2 favor to Kate. I can't stand it! Man, being a twin is the best.
3
4
5
6
7
8
9
10
11
12
13
14
15
16
17
18
19
20
21
22
23
24
25
26
27
28
29
30
31
32
33
34
35

Moss-Covered Rock

1   *(Strolls onto stage casually conversing with unseen*
2   *individuals. Over-exaggerated posture of nonchalance)* **Beautiful,**
3   **isn't it? Yes, straight out of a postcard. Tourists come here all**
4   **the time on their way to somewhere else and tell me so. Where**
5   **ya from?, they ask. Here, I say. No, really, they answer. Where**
6   **ya from? No one can believe that people actually live in places**
7   **like this: no malls, no fast food restaurants and no super-**
8   **highway. Just quaint houses and quaint shops and quaint**
9   **countryside. It makes me want to puke just to mess it up. I**
10   **could tell you about every crack in the quaint sidewalk and**
11   **every leaf on every quaint tree. Everyone's always coming or**
12   **going ... but me.**
13   **I've lived here my whole life. Six-o-eight Elm Avenue.**
14   **Mom even had me at home. She couldn't make it to the**
15   **hospital over in Westchester, so Daddy called Dr. Fayston and**
16   **they delivered me right there. It must have been some kind of**
17   **omen. Here is where you're born and here is where you'll stay.**
18   **Now, my best friend, Jeremy, he's lived all over. His family**
19   **has moved fifteen times in his life and he's only twelve years**
20   **old. He tells me about the places he's seen like the Empire**
21   **State Building and the Golden Gate Bridge. Places that I've**
22   **only read about. Heck, the tallest building I've ever seen is the**
23   **First National Bank downtown, and it's only four stories high.**
24   **Jeremy has lived in ten different states and three foreign**
25   **countries. His dad does something with computers, and**
26   **wherever they need him, that's where the whole family goes.**
27   **Jeremy says it's been pretty cool to go to all those places. It's**
28   **taught him to meet new people and try new things. I can't**
29   **imagine eating sushi or humus or plantains or half of the foods**
30   **he's had to eat. The most exotic flavor I've ever tried is**

1   pistachio. Ice cream, that is.
2   Yes, I'm a regular tour guide around here. I can tell you
3   stories about every square inch of this place. About the time
4   Miss Millie lost her fake leg in the library. About the bad
5   sap run in '98. About the annual elementary school pancake
6   breakfast and auction. Things so exciting they'll just about
7   bore you to death.
8   One of these days I'm gonna go across the Putnam
9   County border and keep on going till I'm somewhere else.
10 I'll keep going until I've seen both oceans and then maybe,
11 just maybe, I'll come back here to see what brings the
12 tourists in droves.
13
14
15
16
17
18
19
20
21
22
23
24
25
26
27
28
29
30
31
32
33
34
35

Rolling Stone

1   *(Walks On-stage with a camera and begins shooting a few*
2   *photos before beginning monolog.)* **I'm trying to capture this**
3   **town on film before we move again. I've moved fifteen times in**
4   **twelve years. I've lived in ten different states and two, no**
5   **three, different countries. It's hard enough to keep them all**
6   **straight in my mind, so I try to take as many pictures as**
7   **possible while I'm somewhere. I say while I'm here, because I**
8   **know, sure as I know my last address that sooner or later Dad**
9   **will come home and say "Guess what?" I never guess anymore**
10   **'cause I know what the answer is going to be. We're moving.**
11   **Again.**
12   **   Mom says that I'm lucky to have experienced so many**
13   **things in my life. It's an experience all right. Once Dad makes**
14   **his announcement, the packing starts. After fifteen moves, I've**
15   **learned that it's better to have less stuff. Less stuff means less**
16   **to pack. I pack my photos and books and my compass. My**
17   **compass is the only thing that's really important to me. I can**
18   **live anywhere as long as I have my compass.**
19   **   Once everything is packed, it's time to get going. If we're**
20   **staying in the States, then we usually rent a moving van and**
21   **drive. Sometimes, Dad's company will fly us out ahead of our**
22   **stuff, but not often. Once, we even got to take a train. But I**
23   **never mind the driving because I like to see the sights along**
24   **the way. I keep guessing which town will be mine.**
25   **   After we reach destination number one thousand and one,**
26   **the unpacking starts. Mom complains that she can't find**
27   **anything. My brother complains that there's nothing to do. I**
28   **go exploring. First, I explore the house. Then I explore the**
29   **street. After that, it's time to check out the local mall.**
30   **   Once we got moved to Paris. Sounds exotic, huh? I've**

never been more lost in my whole life. All the bridges and churches and houses looked the same. I couldn't pronounce our street name, and I couldn't figure out the money to make a phone call. I don't think I would have known the number if I could. Fortunately, I stopped a policeman. He spoke enough English to get me home. Now I carry a compass. Dad taught me to use one after I got lost. Even if I can't remember my address, I can always find my way home.

I have to admit that it's exciting to live somewhere different all the time. Mom's right when she says that not a lot of people travel like we do. I've lived more places than most adults. I've learned about cultures and places that most people only read about. I've learned that no matter where you go, people are always the same.

But most of the time, I'd rather stay put. Just when I start to fit in, we pick up and move. I'd like to belong somewhere instead of just visit. When I grow up, I'm gonna plunk myself down in a place and grow some roots. Like the big oak tree outside my new home, I'm gonna be part of someplace forever. Until then, I'm fixing all my experiences on film so I won't forget them. After all, it's gonna be sooner than later that Dad will call us in and say "Guess what?"

Just Another Joe

1   I have the most boring name on the whole planet! Joseph
2 Smith. Isn't that boring? Almost puts you to sleep, doesn't it?
3 Actually, It's Joseph Michael Smith the Fourth, which is hard
4 to believe. I mean, with all the exciting, creative names out
5 there, sticking that boring name on four people in a row
6 should be some sort of criminal offense. Joe is so unoriginal
7 that there are three other guys named Joe in my science class.
8 Three! One of them even has my same last name. Fortunately,
9 he goes by Allen 'cause it'd be just too weird having two
10 Joseph Smiths in the same grade let alone the same class. Even
11 if I went by my middle name, I'd still have the same problem.
12 There are already two Michaels without me.
13   The other problem with my boring name, aside from the
14 fact that it's boring, is that no one remembers who I am. Carey
15 McNeil, the cutest girl on the whole planet, called me the other
16 night. Me! When I said hello, and she said, "This is Carey," I
17 tripped over the phone cord. Well, we talked for a while about
18 school and Mr. Eastman, our science teacher, and then she
19 starts asking me if I'd studied my lines. My lines? Turns out
20 that Carey really wanted to talk to Joe Stevens (He's one of the
21 Joes in science with me) about a scene they're doing together
22 for drama. She wasn't sure what his last name was so she was
23 just calling all the Joes on our team. The next day, all the Joes
24 in science were bragging that Carey called them. I didn't
25 bother. I only want to brag if someone wants to talk to me on
26 purpose. But with a name like Joe, it happens all of the time.
27   There are a few good things about having a name like Joe.
28 Nobody ever says it wrong. Nobody ever spells it wrong. And
29 with a name like Joe, I can be anyone I want to be.
30   There's this girl on our team named Tawanda LeTrec.

1 Now that's a name! But her name gives you a picture in
2 your mind, doesn't it? A tall girl who's exotic, daring, bold.
3 The real Tawanda was absent for the first two days of
4 school, so everybody was curious about her before she ever
5 set foot in the classroom. When she finally did show up, she
6 was as far off from her name as a person could be. She had
7 braces and glasses, and was kind of chunky. Her red hair
8 was the most unusual thing about her, but it wasn't the
9 wild-woman kind of red hair. It was all neat in a ponytail. A
10 really big nerd. I still want to call her Mary.
11   But a Joe like me can be anyone. And that's the best
12 part of being a Joe without a doubt.
13
14
15
16
17
18
19
20
21
22
23
24
25
26
27
28
29
30
31
32
33
34
35

Tawanda LeTrec

1   I don't know what my parents were thinking when they
2 named me Tawanda. When my mom was pregnant, she was
3 going through this "empowerment" phase. She said Tawanda
4 sounded like a strong, adventurous, determined name. A name
5 that declared to the world, "I am woman, hear me roar!" But
6 then I came out. I was skinny and blotchy and had this really
7 pointed head. I've seen the pictures. I don't think I looked the
8 least bit strong or determined, but Mom went ahead and
9 named me Tawanda anyway. I've been stuck with a name that
10 doesn't fit me ever since.

11   I'm not the only one who thinks I don't look the least bit
12 like a Tawanda. Every year when school starts, the teachers
13 always look over my head when they call out my name.
14 They're looking for someone tall, exotic, daring, but then I
15 have to raise my hand. If I had a dollar for every time I heard,
16 "You don't look like a Tawanda," I could have paid for my
17 college education by now.

18   I've tried using my middle name, which is Adele. I look
19 more like a Mary or a Sarah than either Tawanda or Adele,
20 but Adele sounds closer to what I think fits my personality.
21 When I was in the fifth grade, I got away with it until
22 Christmas vacation. But during my mid-year conference with
23 my teachers, I got caught. Mom just about had a fit right there
24 and then. She insisted that the teachers call me Tawanda. Now,
25 Mom makes a point to talk to my teachers at the beginning of
26 the school year, so I don't have a choice. She's always telling
27 me that I should be proud of my name. I'm not.

28   Sometimes, I pretend that I'm the person my name wants
29 me to be. I make my hair all wild and frizzy. I take off my
30 glasses. I put on my skimpiest tank top undershirt and

1 practice saying, "Hi, my name is Tawanda. What's yours?"
2 But I can't do it in real life. I feel like Clark Kent changing
3 into Superman, but I don't feel like *Super* anybody. I feel
4 like a dork. A dork named Tawanda that is.
5
6
7
8
9
10
11
12
13
14
15
16
17
18
19
20
21
22
23
24
25
26
27
28
29
30
31
32
33
34
35

S Is for Special

1   My sister, Sarah, is special. Mom and Dad tell her so at
2   least ten times a day. They tell me too. In fact, I even hear how
3   special Sarah is more times a day than she does. If I'm
4   building a model and Sarah tries helping and it busts, I'm not
5   supposed to yell at her 'cause she's "special." If I have a friend
6   over and she tries to hug and kiss him, I'm not supposed to tell
7   her to get lost or leave us alone because she's "special." Special
8   is Mom and Dad's word for retarded. But I'm not supposed to
9   say that either.
10   Nobody knows why I am the way I am and Sarah is the
11   way she is. Mom says that she did all the same things when she
12   was pregnant with Sarah as she did when she was pregnant
13   with me. It's just the way it is. This year, Mr. Eastman, my
14   science teacher, taught us about chromosomes when he was
15   teaching us genetics. He said that unlike the rest of us, kids
16   with Down Syndrome have an extra chromosome that makes
17   them the way they are. It's a freak of nature and there's no
18   cause. No warning that all those little cells are out-of-whack.
19   It's no one's fault, but that still doesn't change anything when
20   Jill Evans is studying at the kitchen table and Sarah is
21   pretending to be a dog and pretends to pee on her leg.
22   It's not that I don't love Sarah, because I do. She's really
23   sweet and cares a lot about other people. Last summer when I
24   broke my leg skateboarding, Sarah made me this huge "Get
25   Well Soon" card. It was all decorated with seashells and dried
26   flowers and feathers, so I knew Sarah had raided her own
27   nature collection to make it for me. The handwriting was all
28   crookedy but she stayed on the lines for the most part. It made
29   me feel good that Sarah cared enough to spend all that time on
30   me.

1 Sarah also likes to go exploring and she's not all girly
2 weird when you see a frog or a snake and she throws pretty
3 good too, even if she can't run fast enough to beat a snail.
4 Sometimes I let her get to the base and pretend that she's
5 too fast for me, but even Sarah knows better. She just
6 stands there and grins and teases me that maybe I can catch
7 her next time. She can even play a decent game of checkers.
8 So, for a sister, Sarah's great.
9 But when my friends are over, things are different. They
10 act all nervous like they'll catch something if Sarah touches
11 them, and Sarah gets all weird too. Lately, she's always
12 trying to hug and kiss them and it gives my friends the
13 creeps. I don't know how to get her to stop without yelling.
14 That's when I get told Sarah is special. That she doesn't
15 understand. If you ask me, Sarah understands perfectly,
16 and she just likes to see my friends squirm. Or maybe she
17 really is boy crazy 'cause there aren't any decent guys at
18 her school so she has to maul mine instead. Mom says that's
19 not true, but it doesn't make me feel any better. A normal
20 sister wouldn't act like that. A normal sister wouldn't stick
21 her fingers in my friend's peanut butter crackers on
22 purpose. It doesn't make me stop wishing that Sarah was
23 normal and not so special after all.
24
25
26
27
28
29
30
31
32
33
34
35

Handicapable

1   My parents say that I am "special." My grandma says that
2   God gives "special" people "special" children. I say it's crap.
3   It's true that I'm "special," meaning unique, because I don't
4   know anyone else who has CP in my whole school. Still, isn't
5   everyone special? Why am I so much more special 'cause I've
6   got Cerebral Palsy?
7   Mom says I'm perfect but let's face it, I'm not. Not even if
8   you don't count my CP, which everyone does. I move like a
9   spaz and I slur my words when I talk. I have to use a
10   wheelchair and have special grips on my pencils so I can hold
11   them. I'm definitely not perfect.
12   What I am is smart. This year I started high school and
13   I'm one of ten kids in my class signed up for the I.B. program.
14   There are parents who would kill for a kid with my brains, at
15   least most of my brains, that is. Part of them is worthless.
16   Mom talks about my being special more than anybody. I
17   think she feels a little guilty about my CP, not that it's really
18   her fault. She was in a car accident right before I was born.
19   Some guy smashed into her side of the car and pow! I got the
20   real injury. Who knows if that's why I'm really the way I am,
21   but that story is the best the doctors could come up with.
22   Thank God, my thinking brain is fine. But the movement part
23   of my brain, forget it.
24   The fact that I've mentally got it all together makes some
25   part of having CP better. One of the good things is that I get to
26   go to real school and I can participate in a lot of activities. I'm
27   a whiz at debate, I love to read and write, and I'm even a
28   cheerleader. I don't jump around, but I've got pompoms and
29   a uniform and I do what I can. People think that if my arms
30   are flying it's because I'm cheering. Sometimes I am and

1   sometimes I'm not. I've gone to school with a lot of the same
2   kids since I was little, so they're used to me when I move
3   kind of weird.
4   The bad thing is that when I'm not around my friends,
5   family or school, I'm with it enough to know that other
6   people crack jokes and make fun of me. One time, my best
7   friend, Kaitlyn and I were at the mall. This group of guys
8   was checking us out. We were laughing and waving at them
9   when they yelled over to Kaitlyn, "Dump the retard and
10   come hang out with us." People always think that because I
11   have trouble moving that I must be stupid too. It never
12   occurs to them that I could be a real person trapped inside
13   some messed up shell. Anyway, I started crying and when
14   Kaitlyn went over to tell them off, this little girl came up to
15   me. She wanted to know what was wrong, why was I
16   crying? I tried to wipe away my tears but I had trouble
17   getting my hands up to my eyes. Then, this little girl
18   reached out and wiped my tears. Isn't that sweet? She
19   asked what was wrong with me, so I told her. Then she
20   pointed to her knee and showed me that she had a boo-boo
21   too. I wish more people could be like this little girl. CP isn't
22   a disease; it's a boo-boo. I just happen to be trapped inside
23   of it. But there's a person underneath. A thinking, loving,
24   caring person who wants to feel special instead of just being
25   "special."
26
27
28
29
30
31
32
33
34
35

Over the River and through the Woods

1   Lots of kids think I'm nuts, but I love going to my
2 grandmother's house. She lives in this little town on the top of
3 a hill overlooking the countryside. There are other houses near
4 hers but Grandma's got the best view. We live outside of
5 *(Name of big city)* in this one-story house that looks like
6 everyone else's. My mom's decorated it real nice but it pretty
7 much looks like the rest of my friends' houses. I don't even
8 have to ask where the bathrooms are. I can guess just by where
9 they are in my house.
10   Grandma's house isn't like any other house I've ever been
11 in. It was built more than a hundred years ago by my great-
12 great grandfather. It has five bedrooms but only one
13 bathroom. Even my house has two. It's got a lot of other cool
14 stuff though. There's this one bedroom that has a set of stairs
15 in the closet. They stop at the ceiling. It's so weird! There's a
16 side porch that's all screened in, and in the summer Grandma
17 lets us sleep there. The basement has a dirt floor and it's really
18 creepy. When we were little, my cousin George dared me to
19 stay down there for five whole minutes. He accidentally locked
20 the door and my dad had to take the door off its hinges to get
21 me out. I was really scared but I found a coin that turned out
22 to be from the Civil War! Now I'm the first one to volunteer to
23 get something out of the basement. You never know what you
24 might find down there.
25   That's the other thing about going to Grandma's. You
26 never know who's gonna be there. At Christmas, almost
27 everyone in our family drops in but she's got as much
28 company any other time of the year. Last month, my Aunt
29 Casey and my other cousins, Sarah and Steven, were there.
30 My Uncle Bill was going out of town so they decide to pack up

1   and go to Grandma's. The time before, my Uncle Teddy was
2   home from a business trip. He's a journalist and travels all
3   over the world, but since he's not married yet, he stays with
4   Grandma if he doesn't have an assignment. When he's
5   there, he'll take us exploring in the woods or to the old-
6   fashioned movie theater in town.
7   But the best part of going to Grandma's is Grandma
8   herself. She's so round, she's squeezable, and she gives
9   great hugs in return. She always smells like dough or spices
10 from a pie or loaf of bread that she's just made. If a little
11 dirt gets on her floor, she doesn't freak out. She just
12 reminds you in the sweetest voice where the broom is and
13 gives you a big kiss when you're done sweeping up.
14 Whenever I think of the word love, I think of Grandma.
15   This weekend, my friend Chris is going water-skiing,
16 my friend Patrick is going to Adventure Land, but I'll have
17 the best time of all. I'm going to Grandma's!
18
19
20
21
22
23
24
25
26
27
28
29
30
31
32
33
34
35

Do I Have To?

1   Going to my grandmother's house is a nightmare! My best
2 friend has this grandmother that acts like she came out of a
3 storybook. She looks nice, acts nice and has this really cool old
4 house with lots of places to explore. It's the kind of house
5 where you'd expect to find a secret passageway. My
6 grandmother's is the exact opposite. If Tony's family comes
7 from a fairy tale, my family comes from a nightmare!
8   My grandmother lives in this boring old house in the
9 suburbs. It's not old enough to be interesting, and it's not new
10 enough to be cool. She keeps it really dark by hanging these
11 thick plastic curtains over all the windows. She says the light
12 hurts her eyes, so instead she lives like a vampire. Her house
13 smells like dog (even though he's been dead since I was five)
14 and old cabbage. Sometimes it smells like Grandpa, which is
15 worse.
16   Grandpa has this disease where he can't remember stuff
17 so he forgets to take a bath. He has to get pretty stinky before
18 Grandma notices and tells him to go wash. By then, the air in
19 the house is usually tainted. When Grandma opens the
20 windows to air out the place, you can smell Grandpa as you're
21 coming up the walk.
22   Grandpa doesn't do much either. He sits in a chair in the
23 corner and stares at the TV, even when it isn't on. When you
24 try talking to him, he either can't hear you or can't remember
25 your name. Last time we went to visit, he called me Billy. It
26 was so creepy 'cause Billy was Grandpa's brother, and he's
27 been dead longer than the dog!
28   Grandma's house is even worse at Christmas. My Aunt
29 Phyllis brings her kids who aren't old enough to do anything
30 but are too big to be babies. They jump around on all the

1   furniture. I'm supposed to watch them, and if they get
2   really out of control, I get in trouble! My other aunt, Patty,
3   just sits around the dinner table and bosses everyone
4   around. That's bad enough, but when she isn't acting bossy,
5   she's complaining about her headache or her hip or her
6   back. It's enough to give me a headache.
7   I know I should love my family 'cause some kids don't
8   have anybody to love them and my family does love me in
9   their own way. Aunt Patty always tells me how beautiful
10   (handsome) I'm getting, and Aunt Phyllis always pays me
11   for helping watch the little kids. Grandma even cries when
12   we leave. But I can't help wishing that Grandma's house
13   had a secret passageway. Maybe a passageway home!
14
15
16
17
18
19
20
21
22
23
24
25
26
27
28
29
30
31
32
33
34
35

Fantasy Land

1   My mom says that I live in a fantasyland and sometimes,
2   I'd have to agree with her. No matter what book I'm reading,
3   I can't seem to separate myself from the story long enough to
4   come back to the real world. But really, why bother? Look at
5   what the real world has to offer.

6   Last night our teacher assigned us TV for homework. Lots
7   of kids would think that's cool but when a teacher assigns you
8   television homework, you can already guess that she's not
9   assigning any interesting late night TV. No, we were supposed
10   to watch the news report and compare the news story with the
11   same story in the newspaper. First, I got out the newspaper.
12   The big front-page photo was a massive fire eating its way
13   through a mobile home park. Another story was about some
14   serial killer and another about this couple that used kittens to
15   train their dog to fight. Who are these horrible people? Not
16   even the worst storybook villains do things like that! I don't
17   want to read that stuff!

18   After I turned on the news, it got worse. I heard a report
19   about some little kid drowning in her pool during a party, a
20   teacher who got arrested for touching some of his students the
21   wrong way and a horrible accident where this train full of
22   cows hit a school bus stalled on the tracks. What are people
23   thinking?

24   The books that I read always end happily, which is the way
25   the world should be. True love always prevails. Anyone that is
26   lost always finds their way home. In my books, the bad guy
27   always gets what he deserves. But the world doesn't seem to
28   work that way.

29   The next day, I flat out told my teacher that the whole
30   assignment made me sick to my stomach and I refused to do it.

1   I offered to do an extra book report to make up for the
2   missing assignment. My friends said I was nuts, but at least
3   I won't have nightmares! Call me what you want, but I'll
4   take pretend over the real world any day!
5
6
7
8
9
10
11
12
13
14
15
16
17
18
19
20
21
22
23
24
25
26
27
28
29
30
31
32
33
34
35

Just the Facts

1   *(Student walks On-stage holding the* Guinness Book of
2   World's Records. *He does not look up but mutters "Wow!"*
3   *"Cool!" "Oh, man, look at that!" to himself as he walks On-stage.*
4   *When Center Stage, he looks up to tell the audience a juicy fact.*
5   *Note: Most of the facts in this monolog are interchangeable with*
6   *facts of the actor's choosing.)*
7   **This *Guinness Book of World Records* is fascinating. Do**
8   **you know that a jellyfish is ninety-five percent water and that**
9   **it doesn't have any bones or even a brain? That is so weird! Or**
10   **that the oldest goldfish lived for forty-three years? Yup, some**
11   **old lady won the fish at a carnival game and carried it home**
12   **in a plastic bag and it lived for forty-three years. When it**
13   **finally died, she didn't flush it either. She buried it in the**
14   **ground in its own little fishbowl.** *(Consults book.)* **Oh, and it**
15   **says here that a blue whales' tongue weighs as much as a**
16   **Volkswagen Beetle! That thing must be huge! One time, I went**
17   **to the grocery store with my mom and the meat section was**
18   **selling beef tongue. It was really gross but I couldn't get over**
19   **how big it was. And that's just a cow!**
20   **I love facts. I can't get enough of them. Can you tell? My**
21   **older brother got me this book for Christmas and it's made me**
22   **like some kind of facts addict. Thank goodness, my teacher lets**
23   **us choose what kinds of books we read, because I really have**
24   **to struggle to finish some stupid made-up story. But books**
25   **about facts or real things I can read all day everyday. I even**
26   **read them when I don't have to. I read about sports, nature,**
27   **people. You name it. Did you know that Albert Einstein said**
28   **"Imagination is more important than knowledge"? This from**
29   **the guy with the smartest brain on the planet. Or that Helen**
30   **Keller who was deaf, blind, and couldn't talk when she was**

1 little grew up to go to college, lecture and write books?
2 That's amazing! Then there are the not-so-famous people
3 like the Human Cannonball who got shot out of a cannon
4 and flew one hundred, eighty-five feet, ten inches through
5 the air. Or the fattest man who weighed more than one
6 thousand pounds. That's more than half the kids in my
7 English class put together including Danielle Biggins.
8   Then there are the weird facts. Did you know that
9 racecar is the same spelled forward or backwards? Or the
10 Earl of Sandwich really did invent the sandwich?
11   Besides, why read stuff that's made up. The real world is
12 strange enough already. There's this actor who discovered
13 that the fetus of his dead twin brother was implanted in his
14 arm! How gross is that? Imagine waking up one day to
15 discover that you were a twin, he died and he's buried in
16 your arm. You just can't make that stuff up. And that's the
17 neatest part about it. It makes me feel smart to know stuff
18 that other people just wonder about. So just give me the
19 facts, ma'am ... and keep 'em coming.

Trailer Trash

1   Mom, I'm home! *(Student walks On-stage from right with*
2   *backpack or books from school.)* Sheesh, look at this place!
3   Donut boxes, crusty dishes, is that somebody's underwear? I
4   don't want to know ... *(Addresses the audience.)* I'm sorry you
5   had to see the place like this, not that it ever looks a whole lot
6   better. When they're both here, it usually looks worse!

7   Mom is such a pig. All she ever does is sit around on her
8   fat butt and watch Jerry Springer or some other trash TV. She
9   thinks it's real. Like tossing a guy who's a doctor into the
10   audience is real? Come on! If it was a mosh pit at a concert,
11   maybe, but they're grown-ups. They're supposed to be
12   dignified or something. Even I know better.

13   Personally, I hate TV. Why watch other people's problems
14   when you've got your own? Mom's all right most of the time.
15   She does eat a lot, but she's OK. I mean, she's not a bad
16   person. She's just dumb. She smokes, she sits around and
17   complains, but I know she loves me most of the time. Like
18   when Allen Parker stole the chemicals from science lab and
19   then blamed it on me, Mom got dressed and came down to the
20   school and everything. When the principal called me into his
21   office, she said she "brung me up good to know better than to
22   steal." Thanks, Mom. Everyone thinks I'm trash 'cause of my
23   parents so I wished she'd have just kept quiet, but I know she
24   believed me. That's what really counts.

25   My dad, on the other hand, is real mean. Not mean like a
26   snake, but mean like a dog that's been kicked around. You see
27   a snake, and you know to keep clear. But Dad's like that dog.
28   Sometimes he's all friendly and nice and just when you begin
29   to trust him, bam! He goes and rips your arm off.

30   See this black eye? You think I got it in a fight, right? Not

1 the kind you're thinking of anyway. Brought my report
2 card home the other night. I was proud of it and thought
3 that Dad would be too. After all, I got three Bs, one A and a
4 C. So I'm standing there and pow! Outta nowhere comes
5 Dad's fist. Man, my head was spinning. He's shouting I got
6 a D. I got a D in PE 'cause I don't dress out. I told Mom and
7 Dad when school started that I needed a PE uniform, but
8 Dad said he wasn't paying another penny and what do I pay
9 taxes for, huh? So I got a D. I tried to tell him that PE
10 doesn't count, but then he told me of course it counts 'cause
11 it'd make me a man. Who was I? A fairy? Only fairies get a
12 D in PE! When I tried to answer, he popped me again.
13   Mrs. Ashton, my English teacher, is the only one who
14 knows the truth. She's really nice. She dresses neat, like a
15 mother should. She talks softly and looks at you when you
16 talk to her. She looked worried but I know she won't tell. I
17 can trust her. Not like Dad. Not like anyone else. Every once
18 in awhile, I pretend that she's my mom. If she was my mom,
19 people wouldn't think I was trash or look away when I look
20 at them. People would be proud to be with me. If I was Mrs.
21 Ashton's son, I'd stand tall. But in this house, if you stand
22 tall, you'd better be prepared to duck.
23
24
25
26
27
28
29
30
31
32
33
34
35

Living Large

1   Mom? Dad? Anybody home? *(Student walks On-stage from*
2   *left with backpack or books from school.)* Sheesh, would you get
3   a load of this place! Shopping bags, fresh flowers, is this paté?
4   I don't want to know ... *(Addresses audience.)* I'm sorry you
5   had to see the place like this. It usually looks a whole lot better
6   ... Friday is the maid's day off and when she's off, Mom goes
7   bananas.
8   Mom's a decorator. People say she's got great taste and
9   knows all these little tricks that make the difference between
10   showy and showplace. Throw pillows, antiques, knick-knacks
11   and fresh flowers. Those are her favorites. If you hire Mom,
12   that's what you get. Personally, I hate all that clutter. My room
13   is what Mom calls minimalist. I've got a bed, two lamps, a
14   desk and a chair. That's it. I use my closet instead of a dresser.
15   No rugs, no curtains, no pictures, nothing. If I'm not careful
16   and forget to lock my door, I'll come home and find a throw
17   pillow or two on my bed. Mom's always after me to "soften"
18   my room, but why bother when you've got all this? One time,
19   I was supposed to have a parent conference about my math
20   grade, and Mom completely forgot because there was this big
21   sale at Filene's. Thanks, Mom. Everyone thinks I'm from such
22   a good family because my last name is Nicholson, so I wished
23   she'd shown up at least. It's hard to explain to your teachers
24   that your mom's out shopping.
25   Mom does get carried away, but decorating doesn't make
26   you a bad person. My dad, on the other hand, is kinda mean.
27   Not like a dog who's been kicked around, but more like a
28   snake. You see a growling dog, and you know to walk the other
29   way. But with snakes, you never know they're there until they
30   strike.

1 Remember my math conference? Well, after neither of
2 my parents showed up, my math teacher stopped paying a
3 whole lot of attention to me. See, I'm Judge Nicholson's kid
4 and he's sort of well-known around town. He's also on the
5 school board, so most teachers like to stay on his good side.
6 Well, the math teacher, Mr. Anderson, had been tutoring
7 me after school. This year was his first year teaching, so he
8 was trying really hard. He came up with all these crazy
9 assignments that involved food and fractions, and once a
10 week we went outside and did real life math. Do you know
11 that you can figure out the distance from one place to
12 another by using weird angles? Not on paper, but treetop to
13 ground to you kind of angles. It's a little confusing, but I
14 didn't dread going to math 'cause I knew Mr. Anderson had
15 thought of something interesting. After the conference, Mr.
16 Anderson had to stop. His little girl got sick so he usually
17 left early to go home and help take care of her. When I
18 brought my report card home, I had a D in math. Dad
19 called the principal and told him Mr. Anderson wasn't
20 properly seeing to the educational needs of his students and
21 Bam! Just like that, Mr. Anderson was transferred to
22 another school. Poor Mr. Anderson didn't see it coming. I'm
23 getting tutored again, but I bet you I'll still have a D. Mr.
24 Johnson's OK, but he's not Mr. Anderson.
25
26
27
28
29
30
31
32
33
34
35

One of the Faithful

1   … And God, help all those poor suffering souls find their
2   way to Jesus so they might too be saved. Amen.

3   I am one of the fortunate ones. I was brought up to know
4   the Lord. I know that my sinning soul will one day be washed
5   clean as the newly fallen snow, and I will join my Savior in
6   heaven. So says my daddy.

7   My daddy is the preacher at the Mount Holly First Baptist
8   Church. He tells us that it is the responsibility of those who
9   know the Lord to bring home the lost sheep so that they may
10   rejoin the flock. Everywhere I go I'm on the lookout for lost
11   sheep. Daddy calls me his Little Shepherd. Yesterday, when I
12   went to return my books at the library, there was a group of
13   boys standing outside smoking cigarettes and passing
14   judgments on everyone who went inside the building. They
15   called me a rather awful name that I am not at liberty to
16   repeat, but I turned the other cheek as I have been taught to
17   do. They didn't know any better. They were lost sheep for sure.
18   I knew they needed saving, so I walked right up to them. I
19   asked them if they knew the Lord. One of them was trying to
20   be funny and answered, "Not personally." The rest of the boys
21   laughed, but I told them that I did have a personal relationship
22   with Jesus, and he might too if he gave up his sinning ways. I
23   gave him one of my daddy's business cards, which shows the
24   meeting times for the services and invited him to come
25   worship with us. He looked surprised, but then he surprised
26   me.

27   "Are you Zeke's little sister?" he asked. Ezekiel is my
28   older brother, and I'm sorry to say that he is one of the lost
29   sheep. He was a faithful member of the flock until we moved
30   here from Mobile. Daddy felt that the Lord was calling him to

1   the North to spread the word, so we moved to New Jersey. I
2   must admit that I was sad to leave my friends, but the path
3   of the Lord is not always an easy one.
4   Ezekiel started at the high school. It's different here.
5   Kids made fun of his name, his way of talking, how he used
6   to carry his Bible to class. Turn the other cheek, Ezekiel,
7   Daddy said. But after Mama died, he drifted further and
8   further away from the church. I prayed for Ezekiel. Daddy
9   had his new congregation pray for him. He said that the
10 Prodigal Son must find his way home. So far, he hasn't
11 found it yet.
12 I told the library boys that if they see my brother, to
13 please send him home. Until then, I'll keep praying for him
14 and all the other lost sheep to lay down their burdens and
15 embrace the Lord. Like Dorothy said, "There's no place
16 like home." And a home without God, or my brother, is no
17 home at all.
18
19
20
21
22
23
24
25
26
27
28
29
30
31
32
33
34
35

Lost Sheep

1   The sign says "Today's special: Salvation served with a
2 smile. On the house." Daddy's always putting corny messages
3 like that outside of the church. Like it's a restaurant or
4 something. He's no waitress but he certainly can dish up a
5 pretty good load of bull. It's sad that so many people,
6 including my little sister, Ruth, buy it.

7   My daddy's a preacher. He sells salvation. I say sell 'cause
8 there's a price to pay in more ways than one. Every week he
9 sweet-talks these rich old lawyers and bankers to fork over
10 huge lumps of cash. They're so desperate for forgiveness
11 before they die that they'll pay up at any price. Then, when
12 Monday rolls around, they forget the lessons of the Lord and
13 go back to their sinning, thieving ways. Daddy calls it
14 salvation. I call it a crock.

15   My mama taught me to know God. She was good to the
16 core. She didn't need money or even a church to do the Lord's
17 work. She was happiest when she was helping others like the
18 real Jesus. If someone was sick, Mama brought them soup. If
19 a neighbor needed something, hers was there for the taking.
20 She'd do ministries on the street for the homeless. She'd feed
21 them, hand out Bibles and blankets, and make them feel like
22 they were worth something. Daddy preferred to stay in the
23 church, safe behind his pulpit. When they're ready to find the
24 Lord, I'll be here with open arms, he'd say. The only way
25 anyone finds the Lord with my Daddy is with an open wallet.

26   Then Mama got cancer. She tried to keep going, but it
27 slowed her down considerably. Still, she never stopped smiling
28 and never stopped believing in God's plan. But without Mama
29 to guide me, I did.

30   Daddy said that Mama was such a good angel here on

1 earth, that he rewarded her by bringing her to heaven. That
2 line worked with Ruthie, but it didn't fly with me. God let
3 Mama, a real angel, get sick and let Daddy, a salesman, stay
4 alive. I don't want to believe in that kind of God.
5 Daddy thinks I'm one of the lost sheep 'cause I won't set
6 one foot in his church, but I'm trying to live my life to make
7 Mama proud. I'm still mad at God for taking Mama, but I
8 keep trying to live out Mama's work. Even though my
9 friends think it's a little weird, I go down to the homeless
10 shelter when I get the chance and help out. My mama lived
11 for God. Without her, my salvation isn't served with a
12 smile. It's an inedible lump served up cold.
13
14
15
16
17
18
19
20
21
22
23
24
25
26
27
28
29
30
31
32
33
34
35

Dual Book Report: Chester Smartypants and Ima Dunce

1 OFF-STAGE VOICE: Chester, Ima, you're next. *(Two students*
2 *walk On-stage. CHESTER carries a detailed model/poster of*
3 *a volcano. He pulls out a stack of note cards. He is neat and*
4 *well organized. In stark contrast, IMA carries a crumpled,*
5 *torn piece of paper. She is sloppily dressed and fidgets*
6 *nervously. CHESTER sets up the model and walks to Center*
7 *Stage.)*
8 CHESTER: Good afternoon, fellow classmates. I'm sorry
9 that Gerald conveniently caught the chicken pox before
10 his presentation, but like you, I was impressed with
11 Susan's exceptional report on the tsunami. Now sit
12 back and prepare to be startled, terrorized, and awed by
13 the deadliest natural force ... the volcano. My esteemed
14 colleague and I have done exhaustive research to bring
15 you the most up-to-date information on this lethal,
16 natural time bomb.
17 *(IMA freezes, lights spotlight CHESTER.)* Yeah, right!
18 Like I'd ever in a million years willingly pick to work
19 with Ima. Esteemed colleague ... sheesh. Dinosaurs had
20 bigger brains. Ms. Johnson always pairs up the dumb
21 kids with one of us smart kids. We're supposed to
22 motivate them or something. Instead, they sponge grades
23 off of us like remoras. Take Susan and Gerald, for
24 instance. I've known Gerald since the second grade. He's
25 a nice guy, but dumb as a rock. Teachers keep passing
26 him on 'cause his dad is on the school board. He doesn't
27 have chicken pox, but he does have the decency to stay
28 home and let Susan get all the credit, especially since she
29 did all the work. It's not a bad thing to be one of those
30 huggy, let's-make-everyone-feel-smart-and-wonderful

1   kinds of teachers, but Ms. J. likes to raise self-esteem
2   and yell "Great job!" for the easiest thing. After we're
3   done presenting, I bet she'll say, "Great job, both of
4   you!" Why should Ima get the credit? Does Ms.
5   Johnson really think that Ima did any of this? Ima
6   couldn't find her way to the cafeteria after Christmas
7   vacation was over! Ms. Johnson must really expect a
8   lot more from Ima to think she can find her way to the
9   library. I, on the other hand, ended up doing the whole
10   project myself, and Ima gets to feel good about herself.
11   Some deal. *(Lights resume full position; IMA unfreezes.)*
12   Lastly, volcanoes can affect weather all over the
13   world. If several large-scale explosions occurred at the
14   same time, it would change life on this planet as we
15   know it. And now, here's Ima to mesmerize you with
16   the highlights of several world famous volcano
17   eruptions. *(Lights down on CHESTER. CHESTER*
18   *freezes. Spotlight on IMA.)*
19 IMA: I hate him. He thinks he's so smart just because he's
20   got a computer at home. Not everyone wants to score
21   one hundred, fifty million percent on every test or has
22   time for oodles of extra credit. Heck, if I had ten extra
23   minutes to just sit down and rest, I'd probably be as
24   smart as he is. I wish my biggest problem was how to
25   make a volcano for school. My life *is* a volcano waiting
26   to explode.
27   My mom works full-time as a waitress at Denny's.
28   When I get out of school, I have to pick up my little
29   brother and sisters at the elementary school. I have to
30   help them with their homework and then get dinner.
31   Mom comes home about that time and after we eat, we
32   put all the little kids to bed. Then it's laundry or pack
33   lunches or clean the bathroom. By the time I get
34   around to looking at my homework, I'm so tired that I
35   usually only get five or six math problems done.

1	Sometimes I try to finish my assignments in
2	homeroom, but when I'm in a rush, I make mistakes.
3	Mr. Smartypants over there probably has a catered
4	dinner in front of his computer so he doesn't have to
5	disturb his concentration. I bet he's never even seen a
6	frying pan!
7	The worst thing about this type of project is that
8	Ms. Johnson thinks it helps to pair us up with the
9	over-achievers. Like if we get a good grade once in
10	awhile, everything will be OK. Believe me, I'd rather
11	fail with dignity than take a charity grade from
12	Chester here. Some deal. *(Lights up full. CHESTER*
13	*unfreezes.)* And the biggest most famous explosion in
14	the United States was Mount St. Helens. It happened
15	in the 1980s in Washington, D.C., I think. Here's what
16	it looked like. *(Holds up crumpled paper with visible*
17	*pencil sketch.)* That's all I've got. I'm done.
18	CHESTER: You mean that's it?
19	IMA: I was busy.
20	CHESTER: You had three weeks!
21	IMA: I've got important stuff to do.
22	CHESTER: Like your grade isn't important enough? Ms.
23	Johnson, can you grade my half separately?
24	IMA: Shove it, Chester! *(Walks Off-stage.)*
25	CHESTER: See what I've had to deal with? *(Walks off*
26	*opposite direction.)*
27	OFF-STAGE VOICE: Great job, both of you!
28	
29	
30	
31	
32	
33	
34	
35	

The Quiet Type

1   OFF-STAGE: Can you turn the music down? *(Louder)* **I**
2   said *Can you turn your music down? (Walks On-stage shaking*
3   *her head.)* **And she calls that music. Ten drowning cats in a**
4   **barrel would have better harmony ...**
5   I don't know why all grownups think that all kids like to
6   listen to music, especially loud music. I sure don't. If the song
7   is really good and has a nice catchy beat, I may adjust the
8   volume a little bit. But loud doesn't make it better. It just
9   makes it loud. What's the purpose of volume so loud that
10   you'll be deaf in a few years or split your eardrums from bass
11   overkill? Level it out, will you! I'm the kind of person who still
12   likes to hear herself think.
13   Mom's just the opposite. Everything is the louder the
14   better. Loud music. Loud wallpaper. Loud clothes. She talks so
15   loud that I'm embarrassed to bring my friends over. *(Imitates*
16   *in a very loud voice.) So, you're Judy. I've heard so much about*
17   *you from Susan. Do you girls need a snack? (Resumes normal*
18   *voice.)* Yeah, Mom, that would be great. I'll have the Helen
19   Keller Special with a side of Miracle Ear. But it's not just the
20   volume that gets me. It's all the talking that goes with it.
21   I've always been the quiet type. It's just easier that way.
22   What's the use of competing with the rest of my family? My
23   sister is one of those cheerleading types: loud, bouncy and
24   popular. My brother has an opinion about everything and
25   shares it at the top of his lungs to make a point. Dad's a lawyer
26   and does a lot of talking of his own. Mom's a regular mega-
27   mouth. Mom can talk a mile a minute, about any subject, at
28   any time. If there were such an award for a champion talker,
29   my mom would be it. Then there's me. Teachers at school are
30   always surprised to find out who my brother and sister are.

1   No, Mr. Teacher person, you're right. I'm not like them. I
2   am quiet.
3   Quiet people are thinkers. We'd rather take in the
4   situation than try to organize it. People are interesting to
5   watch, but the loud, talkative ones are too busy to notice.
6   Quiet people just go about their business and get the job
7   done. The talkers are too busy to finish. It's not like I don't
8   care or am not interested in something. I've got things to
9   say, but who'd listen? They're too busy listening to
10 themselves.
11
12
13
14
15
16
17
18
19
20
21
22
23
24
25
26
27
28
29
30
31
32
33
34
35

T Is for Talkative

1   *(Monolog should be delivered non-stop if possible.)*

2   I love to talk. Talking is one of the things I do best. *(Waving*

3   *at imaginary character in school hallway)* **Hi, Bobby. Hi, Drew.**

4   *(To audience)* **He is so cute, but I would never go out with him**

5   **this year. He's such a player. He goes out with at least ten**

6   **different girls every year. I was number four last year. He's a**

7   **great kisser. But who wants to be with a guy who's always**

8   **looking out for more? So, I dumped him. All my teachers say**

9   **that I talk a mile a minute, but I can't slow down because I've**

10   **got so much to say. Hi, Gary. He's nice. So anyway, like I was**

11   **saying. I dumped Drew for this great guy named P.J. P.J. is so**

12   **fine. He's all tan and stuff 'cause he's a lifeguard at the beach.**

13   **I really like the beach. My parents have a beach house, and we**

14   **go there every weekend. I've been going to the beach since I**

15   **was five when we moved here from New York. Have you ever**

16   **been to New York? It's really great. Everybody talks fast in**

17   **New York. Anyway, at my fifth birthday party, my parents**

18   **hired this guy to give pony rides to all the kids, but when it was**

19   **my turn, I ran away and hid in my closet. My closet is so full**

20   **of stuff that I couldn't get in there now if I tried. I have about**

21   **a hundred million pairs of shoes. I like to go shoe shopping**

22   **when I'm depressed, but I hardly ever get depressed anymore**

23   **since I started ninth grade. Ninth grade rules 'cause you're**

24   **like with all the high school kids now. I've got to be careful not**

25   **to talk about P.J. 'cause my parents don't want me going out**

26   **with high school guys, which is so weird because ninth grade**

27   **is high school. But he's so fine that it's hard not to talk about**

28   **him. My parents are weird. Who do they want me to date?**

29   **Middle school boys? Middle school boys are babies. Speaking**

30   **of babies, my mom is pregnant. Can you believe it? A baby at**

1   her age? But I love babies. I really like to babysit so I guess
2   I won't mind. One time when I was babysitting this little
3   girl named Ashley, she threw up all over herself and her
4   bed. It was totally gross, but I took care of her 'cause she's
5   only little and you like can't help getting sick all over when
6   you're little. Last year in fourth period, Jennifer K. got sick
7   all over her desk. Right in the middle of class. She just
8   raised her hand to ask to leave but then blech! She ralphed
9   all over her desk instead. It was soooo gross. I would've
10 died. The only time I don't talk so much is when I'm sick.
11 When I'm sick, I just want to be home with my mom and let
12 her take care of me. She makes me toast and brings me
13 ginger ale. Now Mom's always sick so I have to make her
14 drink soda to calm her stomach. Usually I like cherry soda
15 but when you're sick, you can't drink anything like that. Hi
16 Gwen. *(Lowers voice.)* That girl is always sick. She's missed
17 months and months of school so far. Mom always makes me
18 go to school now. I never want to miss that much school
19 anyway. You get bad grades and your parents get upset and
20 then you get grounded and miss out on all the fun. Like next
21 week, our civic club is going to sponsor a car wash at the
22 bank. All the money goes to buy books for the elementary
23 school library. We get to wear bathing suits and we'll have
24 water fights in between scrubbing people's cars. I can't wait
25 to see Eddie in a bathing suit. He's like a movie star he's so
26 cute. I'd bet he'd be a big star, but he's into nerdy things
27 like chess and physics. What a waste! Speaking of waste, I
28 have to go to gym. It's the biggest waste of time. Not to
29 mention, I have to wear a PE uniform. If P.J. saw me in my
30 PE uniform, I'd just die! Talk at cha' later!
31
32
33
34
35

My Favorite Season: Spring

1   *(Student enters dressed in clothes indicative of spring, holding*
2   *flower.)* **Don't you just love spring? It's my favorite season. I**
3   **love the smell of wet dirt. I love looking for Easter eggs. I love**
4   **watching baby animals stumble around on their wobbly new**
5   **legs. I love the newness of spring. It's like a present waiting to**
6   **be opened. Just like a seed.**
7   **All winter long, I look through seed catalogs. Even though**
8   **the trees are bare and the ground is frozen and covered with**
9   **snow, I'm already planning my garden. Each year I try**
10 **something new. Last year I planted nothing but red flowers.**
11 **The year before it was all pinks and purples. This year, I've**
12 **decided to plant a rainbow. All I have to do now is wait for a**
13 **sign that it's finally on its way.**
14 **I didn't always garden. When I was little, I hated to be**
15 **outside. I didn't like the dirt. I didn't like the bugs, and I hated**
16 **to get sweaty. But one spring, my grandmother changed all of**
17 **that. She gave me a seed catalog and a trowel for Christmas.**
18 **At first, I thought it was a dumb present. Even if I had wanted**
19 **to, I couldn't have used it right away. She showed me all of the**
20 **beautiful flowers I could grow, and told me what a shame that**
21 **they wouldn't get planted. She couldn't garden anymore**
22 **because of her arthritis. She even had the nerve to say that I**
23 **probably couldn't do it. Well, nothing makes me want to do**
24 **something like someone telling me I can't. So I did. I picked**
25 **out seeds, and waited for the ground to thaw. Grandma told**
26 **me to be patient, that spring would come when it was good and**
27 **ready. Then one morning, it came! The air was warm, the**
28 **breeze smelled fresh, and I knew the time had come to plant**
29 **my first seeds. Grandma's arthritis wasn't bothering her that**
30 **day so she showed me how to loosen the soil, dig the holes and**

1   plant my seeds. I planted a daisy. It died. But I kept
2   planting my seeds until something lived. Now, I'm an old
3   pro, and can grow just about anything. Grandma's arthritis
4   hasn't bothered her again, so we spend our time in the
5   garden. I love all of the flowers I grow but for me, spring
6   will always look like a daisy.
7
8
9
10
11
12
13
14
15
16
17
18
19
20
21
22
23
24
25
26
27
28
29
30
31
32
33
34
35

My Favorite Season: Summer

1 *(Student enters with summer clothes, holding beach ball or*
2 *fishing pole.)* **The best part of summer is everything. Wait a**
3 **minute. I take that back. The very best part of summer is not**
4 **having to go to school so you can do everything. The whole**
5 **time it's spring, I can hardly wait for that magical day:**
6 **Memorial Day. It's like the unofficial start of summer. Dad**
7 **hauls out the grill, Mom cleans off the patio and I uncover the**
8 **pool. Even if the water is still too chilly to take a swim, I clean**
9 **it out anyway. Just having it ready and waiting is like a**
10 **reminder that summer is right around the corner. June creeps**
11 **in, Mother Nature turns up the heat a notch or two, and**
12 **finally, it's the last day of school. The bell rings, I toss my**
13 **notebooks in the trash, and run out the double doors before**
14 **anyone can call out "Have a great summer!" After months of**
15 **bells and bedtimes, buses and books, there's nothing but days**
16 **and days of nothing to do.**
17 **Each day is like a holiday. One day it's the beach; the next**
18 **day it's fishing off the Main Street Bridge. I like having**
19 **nothing more difficult to think about then should we bring**
20 **deviled eggs to the Stanton's picnic or potato salad instead. It's**
21 **a nice break from history dates and chemical formulas.**
22 **My family always goes someplace cool for vacation too.**
23 **Last year, we went to Disney World. The year before that it**
24 **was the Grand Canyon. This year we're going to be city**
25 **slickers and go see the Big Apple. We're gonna climb all the**
26 **way to the top of the Statue of Liberty and then go even higher**
27 **in the Empire State Building. I'm gonna get to ride a subway**
28 **and go see a real live show on Broadway. On the way home,**
29 **we're going to stop in Washington, D.C. for the Fourth of July.**
30 **I'm a little sad about missing our annual block party, but the**

1   **Fourth of July in the nation's capital will be a blast. They**
2   **spend millions on fireworks just for this one night!**
3   **After we get home, it'll be back to the same old routine.**
4   **Endless nothing. But isn't that what summer's all about?**
5
6
7
8
9
10
11
12
13
14
15
16
17
18
19
20
21
22
23
24
25
26
27
28
29
30
31
32
33
34
35

My Favorite Season: Autumn

1   *(Student enters in school clothes with backpack.)* **Autumn**
2   **only means one thing: school. Oh sure, the first day is kind of**
3   **neat but after that it's just days and days of useless facts**
4   **lumped together. It drives me crazy to sit inside and listen to**
5   **some teacher yammering on about proper nouns or x equals**
6   **something when I know that outside, the world is just bursting**
7   **into color.**
8   **One of my favorite things to do in the fall is to walk in the**
9   **woods. I like seeing all the baby animals in the spring, and the**
10   **woods are nice and cool in the summer, but autumn in the**
11   **woods is almost ... holy.**
12   **The trail crackles with every step. I love the dry shoosh,**
13   **shoosh sound when you scuffle through a big pile of fallen**
14   **leaves. The air is crisp and clear. That chill means no more**
15   **mosquitoes, but a sweatshirt is enough to keep you warm. The**
16   **smell of the wood smoke is like incense and high above you,**
17   **like a cathedral, are the trees. The sunlight makes them look**
18   **like stained glass. The deep reds, the golden yellows and the**
19   **orange. One time I saw this tree all by itself in the middle of a**
20   **field. It was as orange as a pumpkin in front of the bluest sky.**
21   **It was so beautiful that cars had pulled over to the side of the**
22   **road just to look at it. So, when I come across an orange tree**
23   **in the woods, it always reminds me of that lonely field tree. It**
24   **makes my heart hurt to see so much color up close. It's as if**
25   **God himself kissed the tree into splendidness.**
26   **Autumn is also the start of the holidays. When you get to**
27   **Halloween, you know you're almost to Christmas. I love**
28   **dressing up in the spookiest costume I can find. Some guys go**
29   **for gore; I go for spooky. When the moon is full and the bare**
30   **trees look like skeletons, spooky fits in better with the whole**

1 scene.
2   School, on the other hand, takes the fun out of fall. We
3 can't dress up. We can't read spooky stuff. We can't even
4 call it Halloween. They have a Fall Festival, but why
5 celebrate colored paper leaves when Mother Nature has
6 perfected the real thing? Leave it to school to ruin a
7 perfectly wonderful season just by opening its doors.
8
9
10
11
12
13
14
15
16
17
18
19
20
21
22
23
24
25
26
27
28
29
30
31
32
33
34
35

My Favorite Season: Winter

1 *(Student enters in winter clothes.)* **Isn't winter just … just …**
2 **magical? This is the only time of year when even the ordinary,**
3 **ugly things in life are beautiful. Take this trash can, for**
4 **instance. A couple of days ago it was a rusted barrel of bottles;**
5 **now it's sculpture. This tree, bare and ugly; now it's a fairy**
6 **paradise.**
7   **The winter isn't just pretty. Things are quieter in the**
8 **winter too. The snow soaks up the sound. It makes me think of**
9 **Mother Nature as well, sort of like a mother. Sssh! She says.**
10 **The baby plants are sleeping. Be quiet. They need their rest for**
11 **spring.**
12   **Everyone has more respect for Mother Nature when it's**
13 **freezing. Oh sure, you can complain about the heat of summer**
14 **or the rains in the spring. Fall has its beautiful days, but when**
15 **Mother Nature dumps two feet of snow on your town, during**
16 **a winter blizzard, you have to take notice!**
17   **Kids always notice snow first. Though I'm the snow**
18 **shoveler at our house, I'm always happy when it snows. I love**
19 **to make snowmen and snow angels, forts and tunnels.**
20 **Sledding, skiing, snow ice cream. I can't think of any other**
21 **food that my parents would let me play with before I eat it. I**
22 **stay outside until my teeth chatter, and I can't feel my feet.**
23   **But I love coming inside from the cold. It's like a vacation**
24 **to Hawaii. The heat always makes my eyes water, but there's**
25 **nothing like wrapping in a snuggly blanket after freezing your**
26 **buns off for hours. Once I'm inside, I like to sit in front of the**
27 **fire with my cup of hot chocolate and watch the night come.**
28 **The world quiets down, and the sunset makes the snow**
29 **sparkle. I don't even mind when my family joins me. It's like**
30 **family togetherness is part of winter. It feels cozy and safe. We**

1   all cuddle up and watch the snow fall. Snow is peace sifting
2   down from the clouds. All cuddled together, we wait and
3   watch for spring.
4
5
6
7
8
9
10
11
12
13
14
15
16
17
18
19
20
21
22
23
24
25
26
27
28
29
30
31
32
33
34
35

Who We Were...

The New World

1   *(Actor takes careful steps onto stage clutching skirt as if*
2 *wading or stepping in puddles. When Center Stage, takes final*
3 *dramatic step and looks to the audience.)* **America. My new**
4 **home.** *(Kneels to grab handfuls of imaginary "dirt," hugs it to*
5 *chest and rolls about with excitement. In a moment, she looks*
6 *around nervously, hastily stands up and brushes herself off.)* **I**
7 **can't believe we're finally here! Look at this place. Did you**
8 **ever see a place more wonderful? Heaven couldn't be more**
9 **inviting to a weary traveler. Oh, the possibilities of a new land;**
10 **virgin soil waiting expectantly like a true believer at the gates**
11 **of Heaven. I must confess to thee that the possibility of it**
12 **makes me want to dance and shout with glee.** *(Twirls around.)*
13 **But I will not, for I, Felicity Williams, was most certainly**
14 **brought up better … I pray thee, do not tell of my misconduct**
15 **here, will you, my friend? 'Tis only the excitement and joy I**
16 **feel for this new world. I would hate to begin my new life in**
17 **shame.**
18   **When Father told us that Mr. Thompson had secured a**
19 **ship to bring us passage to the New World, I greeted the news**
20 **with high spirits. My brother, John, whooped and hollered as**
21 **boys tend to do, but 'tis not proper for a young lady to do so.**
22 **Not like you've seen here. You won't tell, will you?**
23   **I'd never been traveling before, so the prospect of a long**
24 **sea voyage aboard the Mayflower was a treat to be enjoyed.**
25 **There were many who thought the journey harsh, but I merely**
26 **looked at each new turn of events as a new adventure. Though**
27 **the seasickness did seem to affect many, I was one of the**
28 **fortunate ones who acquired "sea legs" as the sailors called it.**
29 **The food was bland, but there were only a few bugs. The water**
30 **turned, but beer was plentiful. God chose to stir the seas with**

1   his almighty hand many a time, but the rocking merely put
2   me to sleep. Aboard ship, there was plenty of entertainment.
3   Prudence and I would stroll the upper deck or Father
4   would read to us from his great Bible. Everyone enjoyed the
5   songs praising the Almighty, and I would listen eagerly to
6   the men tell stories of the new world. Here, we would make
7   a new start for ourselves away from the watchful eye of the
8   King. Each night when the weather was permitting, I would
9   stand at the bow of the boat and strain for the first glimpse
10 of America. The air was most certainly brisk, but every
11 lurch of the boat brought us one step closer to ... home.
12   And now we're here. After sixty-six days of waiting, our
13 new life is to begin afresh. *(Falls to knees in fervent prayer.)*
14 Lord, thank thee for guiding this stout ship to calm and
15 friendly waters. Watch over us and guide us with a loving
16 hand so that our new life is made in thine own image. One
17 question, Lord ... how does one begin?
18
19
20
21
22
23
24
25
26
27
28
29
30
31
32
33
34
35

The Savage Land

1   'Tis a mistake I tell thee. This foolhardy notion about
2 starting our lives over in a new land. If Father were privy to
3 my thoughts, I'd surely be whipped! You, my dear friends, you
4 will not speak a word, will you? 'Tis a grave sin to go against
5 thy mother and father. The Bible tells us so. But, oh, how I
6 wish we were home. Bound for England or bound for Holland
7 but bound for home.
8   'Tis true that our godly ways made times hard. 'Twas
9 against the laws of the King to not attend the King's church,
10 so many of the faithful suffered horribly under the King's
11 iron-fisted reign. 'Tis written that the Lord will punish the
12 corrupt. Father wanted us safe from his Almighty's wrath, and
13 in this, bought passage to the new world aboard the
14 Mayflower. I dare not say the words out loud, but I could not
15 help wondering could we not find a safe harbor just a bit
16 closer to home? But Father was resolute ...
17   The Lord did seem to be testing our faith. The trip to
18 America was fraught with peril. We had to sleep on the floor
19 like animals. We wore the same clothes day in and day out.
20 Sixty-six days without changing a petticoat! The water went
21 bad, the main beam cracked! Oh, I was certain that the Lord
22 was angry with us for leaving. Father tried to reassure Mother
23 and me, but I'll admit to much doubt. The sailors were a rough
24 lot. They taunted us with horrible names, like puke-stockings,
25 and made fun of our clothes and our prayers. It would do them
26 good to kneel down before the Lord and give thanks for his
27 blessings. Day after day, the water stretched beyond the bow.
28 Even the blue sky seemed like an extension of the water. Then,
29 when I feared that I couldn't take another day of seasickness,
30 the captain spotted land. Sixty-six days, I tell thee. Everyone

1   was joyous. Father even picked up Mother and swung her
2   around! I was shocked. What would the other passengers
3   think?
4   Our joy was brief. The sky was gray, and the land was
5   cold and unfriendly. The trees stood guard on the shore like
6   tall, menacing soldiers. I even heard tell that there were
7   savages in the woods. Half-dressed men with painted faces
8   and deadly weapons. Women and children had to remain on
9   board, and while I was desperate to run free, I was terrified
10   by the thought of living in this wild place. Oh, why were we
11   not at home?
12   Father was anxious to move our family off the boat and
13   into our small home. Since winter was fast approaching,
14   Thomas Arber, the blacksmith apprentice, was to live with
15   us. Though he was a pleasant storyteller, it was tedious to
16   share such close quarters with strangers. 'Tis not a
17   Christian thought to not want to help thy neighbor but I had
18   enough of cramped and crowded aboard the Mayflower.
19   Now a sickness has taken a hold of the settlement. It
20   seems likely that more than half will be dead by the first
21   crocus. Mother was taken to the angels not four nights ago.
22   I am without faith. I am cold and hungry, and my sadness
23   claws at my heart like the starving wolves I hear in the
24   woods. Father says that all of this is a part of God's plan. He
25   says to be strong and to lay my trust at the feet of the Lord.
26   I am willing, but sadly, all I can think of is all that I have
27   lost. Home.
28
29
30
31
32
33
34
35

Live Free or Die!

1   *(Screams and cheers heard off-stage. A group of boys with*
2   *painted faces, dressed in war bonnets and other Indian garments*
3   *run across the stage. The mood is victorious. One young man stays*
4   *Center Stage as the others run off.)* **What a night! Mother feared**
5   **for Father and me, but, as luck would have it, there was no**
6   **need for worry at all. Father consoled Mother by saying that**
7   **it was better to be involved in rebellion than revolution, so we**
8   **were able to take part in the raid on Griffin's Wharf.**

9   **'Twas a splendid escapade. About fifty of us, led by Mr.**
10   **Adams, convened at the wharf shortly after nightfall. After**
11   **dividing our painted lot into three groups, we made our way to**
12   **the British ships docked nearby. Upon entering the Darmouth,**
13   **our party set about uncrating the large stores of tea. We did no**
14   **harm to vessel or rigging, but I'm afraid the teas suffered**
15   **greatly. I, myself, split more than ten chests of Darjeeling**
16   **before dumping them into the harbor below. Each man was so**
17   **focused on his work that nary a word was spoken. It was a**
18   **most silent enterprise indeed. Though I knew Father was**
19   **among the fifty, I knew no other participant save Mr. Adams,**
20   **for the men were most cleverly disguised. Father swore me to**
21   **secrecy bidding me to keep silent as well. If Admiral Montague**
22   **or his men knew our identities, we would put our families and**
23   **our own lives at great risk. Such acts of defiance against the**
24   **King are considered treason.**

25   **As the last chests were being broken, a war cry rang out**
26   **from one of the men. He called "East Indian" and though he**
27   **spoke, I would be hard-pressed to identify him based solely on**
28   **voice alone. Captain O'Connor was caught filling his pockets**
29   **with scattered tea leaves, as were other spectators. O'Connor**
30   **was stripped of his jacket and his pride before being thrown**

1 off the ship in disgrace. I am saddened that his convictions
2 lacked the fortitude to withstand the temptation of the
3 trampled leaves, but I was proud that I was among those
4 who resisted the pungent smell even as I helped sweep the
5 ship's deck of any remnants.
6   After disposing of the tea, we marched back through
7 town in step to fife and song past Admiral Montague's
8 home. Montague taunted us with threats that we'd have to
9 "pay the fiddler yet!"
10   King George may be a fine fiddler back in England, but
11 just as a dog may ignore a flea until it bites, King George
12 will learn that the colonies will not endure further taxation
13 without representation. He will meet our demands. We will
14 live free or die!
15
16
17
18
19
20
21
22
23
24
25
26
27
28
29
30
31
32
33
34
35

Long Live the King!

1   *(Solemn young man walks On-stage. he notices a pamphlet on*
2   *the ground, picks it up, examines and reads it briefly. Shakes his*
3   *head and continues walking.)* **Foolishness, plain foolishness.**
4   **Last night's fracas will certainly have the King up in arms.**
5   **Why, it wouldn't surprise me if his majesty personally**
6   **boarded a ship to sail for the colonies to put a stop to this**
7   **nonsense once and for all. Father says that the patriots act like**
8   **unruly children in need of a sound whipping. After dumping**
9   **all of our tea, they need to be taught a good lesson. King**
10   **George and his men are just the lot to do it. After all, the**
11   **British army is the greatest army in the world. How could a**
12   **bedraggled band of upstart farmers match wits and skill with**
13   **the precision and munitions of the King's own? It's time they**
14   **learned that the King has a right to rule in the manner that he**
15   **best sees fit. That's why he is the King! His rule was**
16   **preordained by God. If God, in his infinite wisdom, sent the**
17   **colonies such a powerful leader, it must be for a very good**
18   **reason. Who are we to question it?**
19   *(Holds up pamphlet.)* **This pamphlet says to join and band**
20   **against the King's men. To establish a new independent**
21   **nation. Independent? My father says, "Independence at a time**
22   **like this is like burning down a house before building**
23   **another."**
24   **I can't imagine what our lives would be like if the King**
25   **chose to abandon our colony. Where would we get supplies?**
26   **Who would protect us? There are the Indians and the French**
27   **invaders to consider. Who knows who else may follow the trail**
28   **when they catch the scent of the orphaned colony? Farmers**
29   **and field hands? Blacksmiths and barbers? His majesty might**
30   **be strict, but better he who has reigned for years than a**

1   defenseless government run by rich patriots.
2   Unfortunately, rebellion is spreading like wildfire. It's
3   no longer safe to publicly support the King. Just the other
4   night, one of our neighbors was tarred and feathered for
5   denouncing the tea raid. Father is already arranging for a
6   safe house with some friends outside of the city. As the
7   "fire" spreads, it will become more deadly. For the safety of
8   our family, Father refuses to stand in the fire's path despite
9   his loyalty to the King. As for myself, I'm hoping that King
10   George will somehow manage to extinguish the flames
11   before it's too late.
12
13
14
15
16
17
18
19
20
21
22
23
24
25
26
27
28
29
30
31
32
33
34
35

Lilly White

1   *(Student strolls onto stage using an umbrella to shade herself*
2   *from the "sun." Wanders aimlessly about until she stops and*
3   *stares off into the distance. Note: monolog should be delivered*
4   *with a genteel Southern accent if possible.)* **Sometime, I stare**
5   **down the hill into the slave quarters and wonder what goes on**
6   **there. Certainly, I've heard stories from Papa and Joshua. Did**
7   **you know that they sleep on the ground like animals? Or that**
8   **they jump a broomstick and pretend that they're married?**
9   **The only thing they're good for is to work in the fields and**
10   **make babies. Father is always happy to hear about new babies**
11   **in the quarters, because they make him more money when the**
12   **babies grow up. They breed like rabbits in a hutch, but rabbits**
13   **are smarter. Negroes are so stupid that if responsible white**
14   **folk like Papa didn't keep them in line, they'd wander all over**
15   **the South like a plague of locusts. Papa and Joshua like**
16   **nothing better than to sit at the dinner table and discuss the**
17   **day's events, but I'm not interested in life at the plantation.**
18   **I'm bored to tears living out here in the country. Why must we**
19   **live so far from a civilized city? My sister, Annabelle, writes**
20   **about all the wonderful parties and teas she attends. She is**
21   **such a dear that she wrote to ask Mother if I could come to**
22   **New Orleans over the Christmas holidays and visit with her**
23   **and Matthew and little Riley. Mother said that she would**
24   **discuss it with Papa, but her eyes twinkled when she said it.**
25   **When Mother's eyes twinkle, it always means yes! No more**
26   **dirt on my boots or cotton dust on my dresses. New Orleans**
27   **has cobbled streets and tall houses and elegant carriages and**
28   **house slaves that know when to keep quiet** *(Looks over her*
29   *shoulder Off-stage.)*
30   **One day, I overheard old Becky telling Tessie that Mr.**

1 Smith, our overseer, beat somebody terribly for stealing a
2 sack of cornmeal from the storehouse. They were discussing
3 it like Mr. Smith did something wrong. Well, I burst into the
4 kitchen and put them in their place. I told them that the
5 Bible says "Thou shall not steal" and Mr. Smith was
6 administering the judgment of the Lord. Old Becky said
7 that I was as nosy as a long whiskered rat. How dare they
8 talk that way to me! When I'm mistress of my own house,
9 I'll make sure that all of the house slaves are silent until
10 spoken to. They'll say, "Mrs. Thomas Wakefield sure is
11 strict, but her house runs so smoothly."
12 But just yesterday, Tessie told Old Becky who
13 mentioned it to Mother that my dress hems were covered
14 with meadow burrs again and had I been strolling in the
15 garden with Master Thomas again? Mother was furious.
16 She said that it was unladylike to linger with Master
17 Thomas when he comes to do business with Papa. She even
18 threatened that I might not make the trip to New Orleans if
19 I couldn't conduct myself as a lady outside of her keeping.
20 And she had just said that if I found New Orleans to my
21 liking, she'd consider sending me to finishing school there.
22 I'll teach that Tessie to mind her place!
23 Master Thomas is so quiet and handsome. I hear from
24 Sophia, who I trust with my dearest heart's secrets, that
25 Master Thomas already owns some two hundred acres of
26 land. I'm already fifteen years old. I'm practically an old
27 maid! Oh, to be away from Thomas for a year. But I'll come
28 back from New Orleans to be his bride!
29 If you'll excuse me, Mother has just called me in to
30 practice my piano. I must perfect Mr. Mason's latest hymn
31 before she'll permit me the trip to New Orleans. She wants
32 to show Annabelle how sophisticated I've become. Then
33 Tessie can help me sort my things to pack. I'm sure that
34 everything will need a good washing before I leave.
35 Everything.

Black as a Winter's Night

1   *(Student moves slowly On-stage, pantomiming picking cotton*
2 *from invisible plant and putting it into a sack. Effort on task is very*
3 *focused. When student is three-quarters of the way across stage,*
4 *she stands up straight to stretch her back and stares off into the*
5 *distance.)* **Sometimes, Ise stares off at the Big House and**
6 **wonders what goes on inside. What they be doing in there? Ise**
7 **been as far as the well out back by the kitchen when ol' Jed**
8 **plum fell down in the field wit da fever and Ise sent to fetch 'im**
9 **some water. Yes, um, close as the kitchen well buts no furtha'.**
10 **Big House looks mighty proud like a King sitting way up ona**
11 **hill lookin' down on his people. But closed up. I ain't gonna get**
12 **to know that King! They got high yellow coloreds working as**
13 **house slaves so they's neva gonna look twice at me. Shoot, Ise**
14 **as dark as a winter's night with no moon. Kitchen well's as**
15 **close to the big house as Ise ever gonna get.**
16   **Ise born here at Master Johnson's. Don't know nothin' but**
17 **this here plantation. When I was just a little chillun, I didn't**
18 **know better. Me and the others play games out in the dirt in**
19 **front of our cabins. Once Virginia don find an ol' umbrella out**
20 **in the trash heap. We'd pretend we was them fine white ladies**
21 **way up in the Big House struttin' aroun' town. Ise too little to**
22 **know I ain't ever gonna be nuthin' but a slave. Once I done**
23 **and turn seven, outs I went to the fields. Don' have time for no**
24 **games now.**
25   **I been in the field ever since. We start work 'fore the sun**
26 **comes up. They calls it mornin' but it ain't mornin'. Mornin'**
27 **got light. High noon, Overseer calls time and we goes off to**
28 **lunch. Ise always running so's I gets a place in the shade. If'n**
29 **you dilly-dally, you're liable to be eatin' your cornbread**
30 **sweatin' in the sun. We have to eat quick and then it's back to**

1   plantin', hoein', weedin' and pickin' till my fingers bleed
2   raw. Don't much matter. You still pickin' and you pickin'
3   some mo'.
4   When I first start pickin', I could'n hardly pick nuthin'.
5   Now I'm worth 'bout half. I'm to pick half of what a big
6   buck like Willie do. If Willie pick four hundred pounds one
7   day, Ise try to pick two hundred. Trick is not to look down
8   them rows. Ifan you do, why you liable to sit down an' cry.
9   Them rows stretch from one end of the earth to the other.
10   So's when you get to the end, all the choice in the world is
11   nothin' 'cause all you can do is start pickin' down the other
12   side. From sunup 'til sundown since I was seven. From
13   sunup 'til sundown 'til I'm dead as Moses.
14   Sundays is our onliest day off. Then we all goes to
15   meetin' way out in the clearin'. Mammy Quinn tells us the
16   word. She tells us that God will deliver us just like Moses
17   and his people in Egypt. We dance an' sing and feel right
18   proud to be as black as a winter's night.
19   I never thinks to run away. Wouldn't do no good. You'd
20   be brought back with your back so wide open people sees
21   what you ate fer breakfast. They only hang the lucky ones.
22
23
24
25
26
27
28
29
30
31
32
33
34
35

Johnny Reb

1   I never figured Sam to be the one to up and run off. Papa
2 says his letter tells that he's gone to the North to join the Union
3 cause. I never figured on Sam to be an abolitionist.
4   We all played with the darkys. Heck, I liked Tall Dan too.
5 Nobody could catch a mess of fish faster than Tall Dan. Once
6 Sam asked him what his secret was, but all he said was his
7 mama told him to conjure up a mess of fish, and since he
8 always listened to his mama, that's what he did. Still, I suppose
9 that Sam spent more time with Tall Dan than I did. Papa gave
10 Tall Dan to Sam when we turned twelve. He said it was about
11 time that we start acting like men and gave each of us our own
12 manservant. Sam got Tall Dan and I got Jed. I would've been
13 real happy to have Jed's company if he hadn't decided to run
14 off. Papa was furious with me and said he wouldn't get me
15 another till I learned how to get control of my boy. Now that
16 Sam's run off, who's got control of whom?
17   I should have known something was bothering Sam. Every
18 time someone mentioned the war at dinner, he got all fidgety.
19 Last night when we went upstairs to bed, Sam was real quiet.
20 I told Sam that we should enlist in the army. I told Sam that if
21 the Yankees got their way and freed all the slaves, who'd run
22 the plantation? Him? Me? I don't know nothing about raising
23 tobacco and neither did he. The family would starve! Papa,
24 Mama, Little Annie. No, we had to enlist to save the
25 plantation.
26   Then he said he'd freed Tall Dan. Seems Tall Dan put the
27 conjure on Sam. Sam said Tall Dan felt like a brother, and he
28 didn't feel it was right to order Tall Dan around. He said he
29 wanted Tall Dan to like him, not because he had to, but
30 because he wanted to. What'd he want with a black friend? I

1   said. It'd only lead to trouble. Guess I was more right than
2   I knew.
3   This morning, all we found was a note.
4   "Dear family, I hope you find it in your hearts to forgive
5   me. I can't see how one man can own another and call
6   himself a man. I've gone to support the Union. I've gone to
7   become a soldier. May God bless you and keep you safe.
8   Your apologetic son, Samuel."
9   Papa's given me permission to join General Lee's army.
10 We're not supposed to speak Sam's name. Mother is beside
11 herself, but I tried to reassure her. Once we whip those old
12 northern boys, Sam will come back to his senses. But
13 Mother's still afraid. I'm not. Nothing will stop General
14 Lee's army. Not the Union, not Sherman, and not Sam.

Billy Yank

1   I saw my brother today. I didn't recognize him. When I
2 left, we were still boys. These past four years have aged him
3 like an old man. War does that to you.
4   We were marching south outside of Richmond. Our job
5 was to block the roads so that Lee's Rebels couldn't join with
6 other Confederate forces. We were marching double time to
7 make up some distance when we came upon the rear of Lee's
8 Army of Northern Virginia. Our boys captured near six
9 thousand of Lee's own men including his son, Custis. He put
10 on a brave face, but I caught the scent of his humiliation.
11   We camped on the roadside, anxious to reach Appomattox
12 Courthouse first. I'm not certain we knew the end was so near,
13 but victory hung heavy in the air.
14   After we'd finished our nightly rations, me and a few
15 fellows were trading stories about the places we'd seen before
16 the war. All of a sudden, Thomas jumps up and grabs his rifle.
17 I made a move toward mine and the rest of the boys did the
18 same. We could hear crackling branches in the woods behind
19 us when this wild, savage-looking Reb comes bursting out of
20 the brush, yelling, "Don't shoot me! Don't shoot!" This rebel
21 was one of the raggediest looking butternuts I'd ever laid eyes
22 on. His uniform was muddy and torn and from the stink of
23 him, he didn't have proper control of his bowels. His eyes
24 stared out of his sunken face like a skeleton, but there was
25 something familiar about the look. He goes to put down his
26 haversack, which looked about as raggedy as he did, and
27 almost fell over with the effort.
28   Thomas and I moved to help him up. He barely looked up,
29 but then he grabs me and yells my name. I nearly about
30 jumped out of my skin. "Sam," the reb yells again. "What are

1   ya doing in such bad company?" It was the same thing Will
2   used to tease me with when he caught me fishing with Tall
3   Dan.
4   After I'd walked him over to our Lieutenant, Will told
5   me that Father had given his consent to fight for secession
6   after I left. He said they were not allowed to speak of me.
7   In the beginning, Will said he felt strongly about saving
8   the plantation from the thieving Yankees, me included, but
9   after four years of death and dying there wasn't much left
10   worth saving. Last I saw of him, he was eating up his
11   prisoner rations like a dog gobbles down table scraps.
12   Mama would have had a fit if she saw her boy's manners
13   now.
14   As for me, I feel more strongly that every man is equal.
15   I've seen rich men die alongside of poor men. I've seen
16   black soldiers fighting side-by-side with men so pasty pale
17   you'd think they were made of dough. I've seen equal
18   misery and pain all around. Every man dies. God laid down
19   that law of equality before the first soldier ever picked up a
20   gun. The only solution is that while we are alive, we should
21   all be free to live.
22
23
24
25
26
27
28
29
30
31
32
33
34
35

Go West, Young Man!

1   *(Actor walks On-stage with a rough knapsack tossed over his*
2   *shoulder.)* I'll be true to you, Janey. Next time you see me, I'll
3   be as rich as King Midas himself! I'm going to California if I
4   have to walk the whole way! Out there is a land just glittering
5   with possibility, and gold too, and I aim to get me a bushel full
6   of it.
7   Father said it's foolishness and plain out forbid it. Still, by
8   the time morning comes, I plan to be halfway to Kansas City.
9   I've got a strong back, a good head and a pocket full of money.
10   I'm as prepared as the army! Father says that all that's out in
11   California is Injuns and idiots. But that can't be true. Even
12   President Polk himself said that there's veins so rich and pure,
13   why, he'd scarce believe it was true if his men didn't plumb
14   confirm it. If it's good enough for the President, then it's good
15   enough for me.
16   Besides, what's one year of mining compared to a lifetime
17   of working as a farm hand? In one year me and Janey will get
18   married in high style. Janey will be the lady of a fine house
19   instead of feeding field hands day and night like my mother.
20   *(Sets down knapsack and rummages around inside. Holds up*
21   *a small bottle.)* And this here is my insurance policy: Roscoe's
22   Goldfinger Salve. Cost me near $2.50 but in a few months, it'll
23   be worth the investment. You just slather it on, hike to the top
24   of some struck-rich mountain, and then jest roll down the side
25   like a pig rolls in mud. By the time you get to the bottom,
26   you're covered in enough gold dust to keep you living like a
27   king. But don't tell no one. It's got to be a secret. There's
28   enough people headed out West as it is. I figure I'll hook up
29   with a wagon train in Kansas City. I may look small, but I'm
30   a good worker. Solid too. *(Makes a muscle.)* Every wagon train

1   needs an extra hand in exchange for some grub. At Fort
2   Bridger, I'll head off toward the Salt Lake, two-step over
3   the mountains in Nevada and run on down into California
4   and my fortune. You're welcome to join me, but I gotta get
5   a move on. My future is waiting half a country away.
6   California, here I come!
7
8
9
10
11
12
13
14
15
16
17
18
19
20
21
22
23
24
25
26
27
28
29
30
31
32
33
34
35

Homeward Bound

1   *(Actor trudges onto the stage with a knapsack, torn and*
2   *patched. He is stooped over even when pack is lowered. His hair*
3   *is wild. His clothes are filthy. All optimism is gone. Tone is*
4   *discouraged and disgusted.)* **Somewhere on the other side of**
5   **those mountains is heaven; somewhere is my Janey and my**
6   **home. This side is nothing but pure hell.**
7   **Oh, I'll admit I was one of the foolish ones. Rushing in like**
8   **some addled dimwit. But dimwits got more brains that I do.**
9   **Dimwits stay home.**
10   **I hit the trail in Kansas City jest like I planned. I hooked**
11   **up with a nice family, the Campbells, looking to start fresh in**
12   **Oregon. They said they was proud to have me along since they**
13   **had nothing but young'uns who couldn't do none of the**
14   **strenuous work. I ain't kidding you. It was a long, hard walk.**
15   **No, that don't near cover it.**
16   **We roasted the first half of the trip and froze the second.**
17   **When I wasn't so parched that my tongue stuck to the roof of**
18   **my mouth so's I couldn't talk, I was near drowning in some**
19   **river crossing the next. I parted with the Campbells at Fort**
20   **Bridger like I suspected. I hope they found better luck in**
21   **Oregon than I did in California.**
22   **By the time I made it to Sutter's Mill, my money had run**
23   **out along with the soles of my shoes. I loaned myself out to a**
24   **crusty old forty-niner named Brown Billy Burton until I'd**
25   **made me enough gold dust to buy some shoes, a pan and a pick**
26   **axe of my own. I thought I'd be free and clear in about two**
27   **weeks, a month at most. Then I'd high tail it back to Janey in**
28   **time for a June wedding. By the end of that first year, why, I**
29   **hadn't made enough to buy passage back to Missouri let alone**
30   **put Janey up in style. Seems every vein had been picked clean**

1   by the thousands of gold-diggers that crawled over the
2   countryside like fleas on a dog. Most gold I ever saw was an
3   ounce or two a day, but when a cup of flour could cost
4   anywheres up to fifty, I near ate up every bit of gold dust.
5   Now I'm just hoping Janey will still have me. I got
6   nothing but love to give her. I hope that's enough.
7
8
9
10
11
12
13
14
15
16
17
18
19
20
21
22
23
24
25
26
27
28
29
30
31
32
33
34
35

A Woman's Place Is in the Home

1   *(Actress marches onto the stage with a picket sign that reads*
2   *"Vote NO! on 23." Actress chants, "A woman's place is in the*
3   *home," over and over. Finally, she stops to blot her forehead with*
4   *a delicate handkerchief. Note: All mannerisms are very ladylike*
5   *and polite, even when angry. Tone may be angry but posture and*
6   *gestures should be restrained as if exerting great self-control to*
7   *keep feelings in check.)*
8   Oh! Excuse me. I didn't see you sitting there. I was so
9   involved in my defense of womanhood that I completely
10 ignored you. How rude of me! But it is a subject worthy of all
11 of our concentration. Each day those suffering suffragettes
12 manage to sway one more representative, or governor, or
13 innocent schoolgirl with the idealized notion that women
14 should be involved in the politics of this great country. As I live
15 and breathe, I hope I never see the day when women hike up
16 their petticoats and march squarely into the voting house to
17 cast their opinions willy-nilly. This great land was not founded
18 on the daydreams of some schoolmarm or on the thoughts of
19 the average housewife on laundry day! The Lord in his infinite
20 wisdom saw fit to bless the man with a larger brain and
21 ambition. Where would we all be if our forefathers had sat idly
22 by and let the cook and the scullery maid decide the sake of the
23 nation?
24   No, a woman's true right is to be free from the political
25 decisions and monetary responsibilities necessary to keep the
26 country running like clockwork. Besides, who has the time?
27 With home and hearth to manage, the children to school and
28 raise, and the social activities of the community to coordinate,
29 must we really shoulder the burden of running the country as
30 well? And if this atrocity, this voting initiative, heaven forbid,

1   does pass, what, my dear friends, what will the average
2   father and husband do with his time? Would he not feel put
3   out or shackled by the whims of his mistress? Would he sit
4   and enjoy the fruits of his labor reported in the evening
5   paper? I should say not! Why read news that you yourself
6   are not making? The order of things established at the
7   creation of mankind and continuing in harmony for six
8   thousand years would be destroyed. It would be a slap in
9   the face of the Lord to want to change things.

10   My friends, I urge you to vote no on issue number
11   twenty-three. Stand up for the honor and tradition that
12   makes America a nation to be proud of! A nation that keeps
13   its women at home!

14   *(Student marches and chants off the stage.)*

15
16
17
18
19
20
21
22
23
24
25
26
27
28
29
30
31
32
33
34
35

Suffragette – September 30, 1918

1   *(Actress storms onto the stage with "Rights for Women"*
2 *picket sign, visibly angry. She's a bit disheveled: clothes rumpled,*
3 *hair hanging down in pieces. She throws her picket sign to the*
4 *ground and jumps up and down on it. She gives the sign a final*
5 *kick and then wipes her brow by dragging her arm across her*
6 *sleeve. Note: If it can be managed, speech should be delivered*
7 *with a rough accent, possibly Irish or British. Think working class.*
8 *Actress tries to appear ladylike, but her true nature shows through*
9 *again and again. She should appear in stark contrast to "Home"*
10 *picketer.)* **Blimey! After all that, I thought we had 'em. With**
11 **President Wilson on our side, I was sure we was going to win.**
12 **Two votes. Two! You think after the war and all and the part**
13 **we played, you think we'd at least be allowed to vote. We were**
14 **good enough to care for the men folk on the front lines and the**
15 **boys at home too. To do their factory jobs — with guns and**
16 **ammo no less — we think we are gettin' somewhere. Then**
17 **poof! Them fat lot of government bigwigs snatches it back.**
18 **Like offering a handful of scraps to a hungry dog then**
19 **deciding to keep it for yourself. Well, they better watch out.**
20 **This dog bites!**
21   **Seems I was born a Suffragette. My great-bloomer-**
22 **wearing-grandmother was part of the first Equal Rights**
23 **Association Convention back in '69. Had enough of the men**
24 **folk telling her she best marry again after her husband died**
25 **'cause she didn't have the luxury of earning fittin' wages to be**
26 **raisin' a handful of children. Why not, she says? I be willin'**
27 **and able-bodied. What do I need a man for? Grandmother**
28 **said her mama's proudest moment was when she heared Mrs.**
29 **Elizabeth Cady Stanton speaking. Oh, she said she had words**
30 **that made you feel proud to be a woman. Made ya feel that it**

1   wasn't if but *when* women would have the right to vote.
2   Great-grandmother never did listen to the men. Went right
3   on runnin' the store like great-grandfather did, raisin' up
4   her children at the same time. She even let the county
5   chapter of the National Women's Suffragette Association
6   meet in her store when people said she shouldn't — it'd be
7   bad for business, they said. So be it, she said right back. It's
8   that kinda gumption that's stuck with our womenfolk ever
9   since.
10   Grandmother and Mama picked up where she left off.
11 They found it funny that people would think that no one
12 would marry a suffragette. Both Pappy and Father liked
13 strong women. Why should they keep their opinions quiet?
14 They're gonna say them anyway, so might as well count for
15 somethin'. I remember Mama dressing me in black when
16 Miss Susan B. Anthony died back in '06. I was just little, but
17 Mama and Grandmother were acting like a close personal
18 friend had passed on.
19   I've done my part for women's rights too. Mama and
20 Grandmother and I marched in two different suffragette
21 parades, and I even marched by myself in 1912. Mama was
22 busy having Leroy at the time, so she was off the hook.
23 Father thought I was rather young to be doin' marchin' by
24 myself, but Mama told him her sister suffragettes would see
25 to me. I yelled twice as loud as I usually do; for myself and
26 to make up for Mama.
27   And now after everything, it's two votes away. Two
28 votes before I'll have my say as to who will be president.
29 Two votes before I can have my say in court. Two votes
30 before my opinion counts for somethin'. Two. If I knew who
31 them senators were, I'd wring their necks! *(Heavy sigh as*
32 *she picks up sign)* Guess there's nothin' to be done but pick-
33 up where we left off. It *is* not if but when women will vote,
34 and two votes may be closer than you think!
35

Who We Pretend to Be . . .

It Was a Dare!

1   If I could put her back to sleep, I would! I know she's
2   supposed to be a princess and all, but she doesn't act like any
3   princess I've ever met.
4   Let me explain: it was a dare. Gosh, we'd grown up
5   hearing the legend of the sleeping princess in the enchanted
6   castle, but I don't think any of us took it very seriously. We
7   always played outside the castle walls, wrestling, jousting and
8   other princely stuff. Then one day after being unseated ten
9   times in a row, Mortimer got this notion in his head to enter
10 the walls and find out if the princess was for real. We thought
11 he was still a little addled. After all, being knocked from your
12 horse can shake your brains up a bit, but then he pulls out a
13 pair of hedge clippers from his saddlebag. He said they were
14 bewitched by Hilda the Horrible and would cut through the
15 enchanted brambles like a knife through a roast. Sure enough,
16 we were able to cut away the thorns until we could walk
17 through the castle gates. Why climb over the walls when you
18 can walk through like a proper gentleman?
19   Once inside, it was very spooky. Everyone was asleep just
20 like the legend said they would be. Even those people who were
21 in the middle of doing something were sound asleep. We took
22 turns daring each other to run up and touch them. No one ever
23 woke up. We made our way through the castle knocking over
24 knights, arranging the courtly ladies in rather inappropriate
25 poses until we came to this little tower. We climbed up all
26 seven hundred thirty-six stairs. At the top, was a thick oak
27 door. I double-dog dared Morty to open it. He did.
28   The room was hung with tapestries and silks and was just
29 about as fancy a room as any of us had in our own castles. But
30 in the middle of the room stood this magnificent bed, and on

1   this magnificent bed, lay the most beautiful girl any of us
2   had ever seen — sound asleep. Francis dared me to kiss her.
3   Heck, if I was gutsy enough to knock over an armed knight
4   in the courtyard, I could kiss this sleeping girl!
5   I walked right up to the bed. I made a big show about
6   kneeling beside it. All the guys were cracking up, but I did
7   it. I planted a big, sloppy smackaroo right there on those
8   rosy red lips.
9   One minute she's sleeping, the next, she's screaming
10 bloody murder! And her breath! If her screaming hadn't
11 scared me, her breath did. One hundred years without a
12 toothbrush will do that to you. She stands up on her bed
13 and starts throwing pillows at us. I didn't expect her aim to
14 be so good after all that time. She yelled words I wouldn't
15 expect any maiden to know and we all bolted for the door.
16 As we started down those seven hundred thirty-six stairs,
17 we met the guards coming up. They hauled us off to the
18 throne room just as I was saying my final prayers.
19   Mortimer and I and the rest of the boys knelt before the
20 King. "Who's responsible for this?" he roared. I figured
21 that I would be gallant and admit to the mistake. My
22 friends could at least remember me in a ballad. I slowly
23 raised my hand and the King starts laughing.
24   "Wonderful!" he shouts. "I'll arrange the wedding feast
25 at once."
26   Seems that beautiful sleeping girl wasn't just any old
27 palace maid, but the legendary sleeping princess herself! It
28 was only supposed to be a fairy tale! Now I'm supposed to
29 marry that sleeping grouch. And I'm not even old enough to
30 rule my own kingdom yet!
31   If I could do it all over again, I would let Morty take the
32 dare. I wouldn't kiss her even if he triple-dog dared me. Not
33 a kiss on the lips. Not a peck on the cheek. Not in a million
34 years this time! It was only a dare!
35

Sleeping Grouchy

1   (*Actress stumbles in dragging a blanket and clutching a teddy*
2   *bear. She is grouchy and yawns continually throughout the*
3   *monolog. By the end of the piece, she is more awake, but still*
4   *cranky.)* **What a way for someone to wake up! I was in the**
5   **middle of the nicest dream. Granted, it was rather a long one,**
6   **but no one likes to wake up in the middle of a dream. It's like**
7   **having a storyteller stop in the middle of a story. What**
8   **happens next? You never know … I hate that.**
9   **In my dream, I'm looking out the window in a high tower.**
10 **I can see for miles. Suddenly, I hear someone yell my name.**
11 **From far below I can see a man. It's not just any man. It's**
12 **Philip, one of the most handsome groomers in all of my**
13 **father's stables. Even the fillies line up to have Philip curry**
14 **their hair. In my dream, Philip's waving at me. He's tan, and**
15 **strong, and his cheeks,** (*Heavy sigh*)**, so firm and taught they're**
16 **like two rosy apples. His shirt is unbuttoned, his chest**
17 **glistening with sweat. The wind blows his hair back and he**
18 **smiles at me; a row of perfect, uncapped pearls. I eagerly pull**
19 **the pins out of my hair and let it tumble down to the ground**
20 **below. Philip uses my hair like a rope and climbs up to my**
21 **tower window. He presents me with a glass slipper. I put it on**
22 **and pull the other from my pocket. It fits perfectly. Philip**
23 **grabs me and pulls me close. "I knew you were a real**
24 **princess," he says. He smells like fresh hay and sunshine. I**
25 **reach up to touch his face and he leans down to kiss me and**
26 **then …**
27 **WHAM! I'm staring at this pimply, red-haired kid with**
28 **big ears, his nose not inches from mine. Well, I scream!**
29 **Wouldn't you? I'm a sound sleeper anyway, so, like, the last**
30 **thing I remember, before my dream that is, is this nice old**

1   woman teaching me to spin straw into gold. She was using
2   this new-fangled piece of spinning equipment. I must not
3   have been very good at it 'cause I pricked my finger on the
4   spindle just about as soon as I picked the dang thing up.
5   *(Looks down at her hand.)* It still stings too! Anyway, that's
6   what I remember: I'm spinning, then Philip's about to kiss
7   me in my dream and all of a sudden, pimply-face kid! I
8   don't even remember falling asleep!
9   Now my parents are babbling about some broken curse.
10   They're all excited because the pimply-face kid is like some
11   prince and wants to marry me. Me? Get married? I don't
12   even have my permit to drive a horse and carriage yet! And
13   what about Philip? What about my dream? That prince kid
14   woke me up at the nicest part so I didn't even get to see how
15   it turned out.
16   That's it. I'm going back to bed. I'm so tired that I feel
17   like I could sleep for a hundred years. Another hundred
18   that is!
19
20
21
22
23
24
25
26
27
28
29
30
31
32
33
34
35

A New 'Do

1   Yes, Scalp 'Em Beauty Shop? I'd like an appointment for
2 one p.m. It's an emergency. The name's Rapunzael. I want the
3 works — a whole new look. I've got this incredibly mangy
4 mop, and I want to cut it off. Cut it all off. I'm done with her
5 rules once and for all. Who? My mother, of course. Well, she
6 says she's my mother but the rumor going around the forest is
7 that she's a witch. Not that I believe it really. I mean, what kid
8 doesn't believe that her mother is a witch every now and then?
9 She's usually a big sweetie, but this time she's gone too far.

10   Just the other day, we celebrated my sixteenth birthday.
11 Pink cake, pink flowers, pink, pink, and more pink
12 everywhere 'til I thought I'd puke. Does she think I'm still a
13 baby? I'm old enough to go to balls now and drive my own
14 coach if we had such a thing, but that's the problem. She never
15 lets me go anywhere. I never get to do what I want. I feel like
16 a prisoner in my own home.

17   We've lived in the same tower, in the same forest all my
18 life. One-oh-one Enchanted Lane. Mom has a day job, so I'm
19 pretty much by myself during the day. I just sit around and
20 weave or sing or pine out the window for a normal life.
21 Everyday at ten o'clock my tutor, Rumpelstiltskin, comes by
22 to teach me princess posture, grooming and courtly
23 conversation — intermediate level. He stands at the bottom of
24 our tower and calls, "Rapunzael, Rapunzael, let down your
25 hair." I have to heave this rope of hair out the window so he
26 can climb up.

27   I've been growing my hair since I was born. It's a
28 convenient ladder, but I want to do all the things a normal
29 princess does. I can't dance to the newest Three Pigs album
30 without tripping over my hair. It takes forever to pull a tunic

1 over my head, and I always get a headache. Mom comes and
2 goes this way too. Seeing there's no doorway, and I'm the
3 only "ladder," I can't go anywhere. No wonder Mom got
4 this place so cheap! Who ever built a tower without an
5 entrance? When I asked Mom to buy another ladder at
6 Jack's Beanstalk Ladder Company so I could cut my hair,
7 she forbid it! Can you imagine?
8   Because I can never leave, I've never even been on a
9 date. Until the other day, that is. See, Mom told me that a
10 guy was coming to fix the leak in the tower roof and to let
11 him climb up my hair at two-thirty p.m. Rumpelstiltskin
12 had left for the day, so I just sat around staring out the
13 window waiting for Mr. Fixit. He called up promptly at two-
14 thirty p.m. He was heavy but a nimble climber, like he'd
15 climbed up hair all his life. When he got to the window, I
16 wanted to pull out all my hair so he'd have to stay. He was
17 beautiful. He told me that he was a prince in a neighboring
18 kingdom, and his dad wanted him to learn a useful skill just
19 in case the prince-thing didn't work out. He loved to rock
20 climb and sing and dance. He loved the Three Pigs too, and
21 just happened to have a friend backstage at their concert. A
22 B.B. Wolf, or something. Anyway, he asked me to go. I
23 didn't tell Mom 'cause I knew she'd say no. So, you can see,
24 I need you to come here. I want you to braid my hair. I'll
25 have to use it as a rope. Um, three hundred yards? You're
26 right; it is unusual to have hair so long. Yes, something
27 short and chic. I have a picture of an imp from the latest
28 issue of *Popular Princess Magazine*. Yes, that's the one. Can
29 you fit me in? Great. One p.m. One-oh-one Enchanted
30 Lane. Tall tower, new roof. Just call, "Rapunzael,
31 Rapunzael, let down your hair" and I'll hoist you up. Bring
32 your sharpest scissors. By tomorrow, I'll be ready to say
33 hello to the new and improved me. Goodbye, tower. Hello,
34 freedom!
35

A Mama's Woes

1   *(Client gossips with hairstylist during an appointment.)* **I'll**
2 tell ya, Gladys, I just don't know what I'm going to do with
3 that girl. You bring them up, try to teach them right from
4 wrong, and what do you get in exchange? Nothing. Nothing
5 but heartache and more grief than an old body knows how to
6 handle. Why just the other day, Hilda and I were talking about
7 this very thing. Seems she's been having some problems with
8 Glinda. That pretty little good witch keeps flaunting her
9 beauty in front of her sister, Agnes. Makes Aggie just a tad
10 greener with envy than she already is. Hilda says that their
11 pranks have gotten worse too, what with trying to drop houses
12 on each other and all. Hilda's afraid that one of these days, one
13 of those girls is going to get seriously hurt.
14   I have my hands full with just one. *(Interrupts story.)* **Nope,**
15 just a trim today. Ever since I had that last bottle of lizard's
16 breath put on it, it won't do a thing. Now, my girl, Rapunzael,
17 what a sweet child. Prettiest pumpkin in the patch. But, Lord,
18 how that child can whine! Why can't I leave the tower? Why
19 can't I have my friends over? Why can't I cut my hair?
20 Everyday, why, why, why? It's enough to put warts on your
21 nose and hair on your chin, I tell you.
22   I had always wanted a baby of my own, but nature and
23 magic just didn't see it that way. Finally, I had decided to just
24 keep cats when this young couple practically gives me a baby.
25 Wanted to trade her for a head of lettuce, they did. One day
26 I've got cats, the next day, the pot of gold at the end of the
27 rainbow!
28   I should have guessed from the start that I'd have my
29 hands full. Cried day and night. Ate like a greedy wolf, and
30 that hair. Practically grew overnight. It must have been

1   bewitched at birth.
2   Now, you know how it is, Gladys. You raise them well,
3   bring them up right and then sooner or later they get a
4   friend who undoes all of your hard work. So, I kept
5   Rapunzael under lock and key. No, really. I did. It does
6   seem kind of harsh but that child was wild from the start
7   and no amount of daisy petal stew was going to change that.
8   Smashed her spinning wheel when it wouldn't spin. Tossed
9   her harp teacher out the window when he made her
10   practice the scales. Only way I could keep control was to
11   keep her under lock and key.
12   Lately, she's been threatening to cut her hair, and use it
13   to climb out her window. Seems some young prince has
14   been wooing her from below. Craziest scheme I ever heard,
15   but I wouldn't put it past her to try it. She's been trying my
16   patience from the day she was swapped. I love her like she
17   was my own but sometimes, after an especially trying day, I
18   wonder who got the better deal in the trade. Sometimes, I
19   wish I had kept my head of lettuce.
20
21
22
23
24
25
26
27
28
29
30
31
32
33
34
35

Hiding Out

1   So's like one day, Pop says to us, "Georgie, Sal, we're
2   moving. Pack up yer things and get yer butts in the car!"
3   Seems he'd had another run-in with that Wolf fella and like we
4   was gonna have to be in some Witness Protection Program or
5   somethin'. Yup, he packs us up to some godforsaken
6   Nevernever Land, changes our names to freakin' Hansel and
7   Gretel and tells us not to talk to anybody — wolves, fairies,
8   nothin'. We was undercover, ya get me? Pop, he knows nothin'
9   but gamblin' so's like this program makes him some sort of
10   lumberjack. Like Pop would know one end of an axe from
11   another. But it's a real good disguise. Nobody's never gonna
12   suspect that he's like choppin' wood or somethin'. Real good
13   cover, see? But it's not like he was good at it, ya know? Whack!
14   Brush the sawdust off his Armani shirt. Whack! Brush.
15   Whack! Brush. So's it's not like he was getting much done.
16   So's he's not makin' much dough. So's like our stepmother
17   goes out to help him. Now I know she ain't ever seen an axe
18   and what with her nails all done that she's gonna be much
19   help. But they do this 'cause it ain't like they got much choice.
20   Well, anyways, me and Sal, I mean, Gretel, is sittin'
21   around with nothin' to do. We's can't go anywhere 'cause with
22   names like freakin' Hansel and Gretel we'd like look like a
23   couple of fruits, ya know what I'm saying? So's we're sitting
24   around with nothin' to do trying to stay outta trouble but like
25   we're hungry. Name or no fruity name, we's go out inta the
26   forest lookin' to see what's to eat. Now I ain't a freakin' Boy
27   Scout or nothin', but Joey Lemanski back home taught me
28   how to pop birds outta the trees for the fun of it, so's I'm
29   thinkin' that birds taste like chicken. We's walkin' through the
30   woods, and it's all dark and creepy like. I didn't see no birds,

1   but we did see a baby deer. Sal, I mean, Gretel says like deer
2   is supposed to be good eatin'. Now I know I ain't ever seen
3   no deer at Schlotsky's Deli, but I'm hungry. I heave a rock
4   at it, but it just runs off. Then some weird dude in a big hat
5   comes by, and Sal, I mean, Gretel just cracks up. He'd have
6   been laughed outta the neighborhood wearin' them rags.
7   Some little parade of midgets marches the other way, and
8   the last one drops somethin' outta his pack. I picked one up.
9   "Whoa!" I says, "This is a diamond!" We know we jus'
10 found the mother lode, but now's we can't find our way out
11 of the freakin' forest. We walk around for hours. Sal, I
12 mean, Gretel, gets all weepy and sniffly. "Shut up," I tells
13 her, "Or I'll pop you like a baby." She just keeps on that
14 she's hungry.
15   Then I sees it. A whole house made outta candy. Like the
16 biggest gingerbread house in the world. We're thinkin' we
17 must be dreamin' and all, but we runs to it and starts
18 snackin' first on one side and then the other. The ol' lady
19 who looks like Mrs. Sedgewick from back home comes
20 runnin' out wavin' a broom, cursin' the whole time. She
21 mumbles somethin' about good enough to eat, and I'm
22 frozen. Crazies always live way out all alone. She had to be
23 one of 'em. She drags us inside, sits us down and lectures us
24 like Mrs. Sedgewick the time our dog pooped on her lawn.
25 She even took my diamond! Then she locks us up in a big
26 ol' cage until Pop comes searchin' for us. Man, I'm tellin'
27 you. The ol' fruit's one crazy bird. We was just hungry is
28 all ...
29
30
31
32
33
34
35

Witchy Poo

1   *(Actress analyzes herself in a mirror. She checks all angles,*
2   *then looks up at the audience.)* **I ask you, do I look like the kind**
3   **of woman that would eat children? Eye of newt, or toe of frog**
4   **perhaps, but children? Never! I have three of my own in fact:**
5   **Agnes, Glinda and Mildred. Glinda was such a sweet child.**
6   **Always did like pink, that one. Never could get her to wear**
7   **regulation witches' black. Yes, all mine. Now, granted, they're**
8   **witch children and not human children, but I'd expect they**
9   **would all taste the same. Children, witches or not, are all**
10   **sweaty, grimy, salty little things from running around after**
11   **crystal balls or dragons or elves. Personally, I like sweets. You**
12   **may have noticed my passion for all things sugary.** *(Gestures to*
13   *imaginary candy house behind her.)*
14   **My house started out as something different. Oh, I know I**
15   **could have built my house out of straw or sticks or bricks, but**
16   **I was going for the unusual you understand? I sat and thought**
17   **about the things that I liked best, but I kept coming back to the**
18   **chocolate-marshmallow nut bar I was munching on at the**
19   **time. So, then I said to myself, "Hazel, why not a gingerbread**
20   **house with chocolate shutters?" Since I couldn't think of any**
21   **reason not to, I did. It's protected from wolves by powerful**
22   **magic, so I never considered it wouldn't be protected from**
23   **children, and human children at that! Children had never**
24   **been a problem, until** *they* **came into the forest ...**
25   **When Hansel and Gretel moved into the woods, I thought**
26   **to myself, "Hazel, you've always wanted neighbors." Again, I**
27   **like children, so I was looking forward to the visits. But those**
28   **two! Dear me! Seems that the father and stepmother were**
29   **gone all day, woodcutting I believe, and those two ran wild.**
30   **Just goes to show you what happens when you leave children**

1 unattended. They threw rocks at sweet Bambi, made fun of
2 the Mad Hatter's hats, and stole from the seven dwarfs.
3 Rotten to the core, I'm sure.
4   One day, I was sitting down to a chocolate shake,
5 reading an article about decorating with cobwebs in the
6 latest issue of *Martha Slimewart Magazine*, when I thought I
7 heard giggling. Well, I ran outside as fast as I could, and do
8 you know that two of my chocolate graham cracker
9 shutters were missing? I started back inside, but then I
10 heard voices on the other side of the house. Hansel was on
11 the roof, systematically devouring my gumdrop chimney,
12 and Gretel was gnawing on my licorice siding. The nerve of
13 those children snacking on my home! I got my broom and
14 flew up to snatch Hansel off the roof. Gretel tried hiding in
15 the marshmallow patch, but I found her too. I took them
16 both inside, gave them a good lecture about respecting
17 other people's property, then I locked them up in my pet
18 dragon's cage until their parents could come for them. Who
19 knew what other mischief they'd get into if I had let them
20 go?
21   The minute their daddy arrived, the little liars began
22 whining and crying about how frightened they were, when
23 they had done nothing all day but sleep and play cards. The
24 worst part was he believed them and not me, an honest,
25 hardworking witch. "Hazel," he said to me, "them kiddies
26 don't lie!" And so, I've had a bad reputation in the forest
27 ever since. Harumph. Kids these days ... all they had to do
28 was ask.
29
30
31
32
33
34
35

Little Red

1   *(RED comes On-stage with red cape, chewing gum loudly.*
2   *Throughout monolog, she irreverently pops bubbles, smacks lips,*
3   *plays with her gum, etc.)* **Listen, officer, I'm telling ya. The**
4   **wolf's a liar. Do I look like a criminal to you?** *(Bats eyelashes*
5   *wildly.)* **It's all just a big misunderstanding. If you let me talk**
6   **to him, I'll have this straightened out in a jiffy.** *(Aside to self)*
7   **If I ever get my hands on that wolf, he'll wish he'd offered to**
8   **have been my coat!**
9   **See, Granny and me, we had a fight. She thought I should**
10 **be in school, and I thought I shouldn't. She's always after me**
11 **to get an education, get an education. I got ya education right**
12 **here, Granny!** *(Spits.)* **I don't need no stinking education. I'm**
13 **gonna be an actress.**
14   **You think I said "Oh, Mr. Wolf, please help me knock off**
15 **my Granny?" Please, I'm not that good yet, sir. Besides, I**
16 **wouldn't do that to Granny. I love my granny, really.**
17   **Anyway, I run to the meadow to be alone. Wolfy sees me**
18 **all upset and he comes over and starts acting all frisky.**
19 **Running around, tail wagging, like he wanted something, if**
20 **you know what I mean. I told him to leave me alone but he**
21 **kept after me. I guess I just started home 'cause I didn't know**
22 **what else to do.**
23   **By the time I got home, I was fed up. I mean, the nerve of**
24 **this guy following me to my doorstep. Some guys don't take no**
25 **for an answer but this guy seemed like he'd follow me inside**
26 **anyway.**
27   **Granny sees me back in the house with this wolf on my**
28 **heels and she starts screaming about fleas, and who did I think**
29 **I was bringing pets home? She goes for her gun and I start**
30 **yelling, "Don't shoot! Don't shoot!" But Granny sees him as a**

1   new fur coat. Now I don't like this guy following me around
2   but I'm an animal lover at heart, so I don't want him dead
3   neither. Look at the mess it'd make! Well, he goes all
4   nervous and jumps out of the trailer. Smashes the freakin'
5   window to smithereens. Crash! There's glass everywhere.
6   Granny's got a gun and a lunatic wolf streaking through the
7   forest. Officer, I swear on my red cape that's the whole
8   truth. I'm just an innocent bystander. A reporter of the
9   facts. Like I told you, I'm an actress, not a criminal.
10   Besides, who needs a wolf-skin coat when you've got this?
11   *(Indicates cape, bats eyelashes.)*
12
13
14
15
16
17
18
19
20
21
22
23
24
25
26
27
28
29
30
31
32
33
34
35

Devil in Red

1 *(Wolf peeks head out of the curtain.)* **Is she gone yet? Do you**
2 **see her?** *(Aside to self)* **You would think I would have learned**
3 **after that three pigs' incident.** *(To audience)* **About this tall, red**
4 **cape, sinister laugh? You don't believe me? Then you haven't**
5 **heard my side of the story.**
6   **I'm out for my afternoon walk, just minding my own**
7 **business, taking my time to stop and smell the flowers. You**
8 **know, life is too short to stay inside your den and sleep. I'm**
9 **just walking and admiring the day. I'll admit I strayed from**
10 **the path. I saw a field of poppies. Red, red, everywhere. I have**
11 **a passion for all things red. So, there I was wandering amidst**
12 **the poppies when this little girl wearing a red cape comes**
13 **crashing through the woods into the field. Running like she**
14 **was being chased by a troll and three bears. She's running and**
15 **crying and falls down in the middle of all those flowers. I have**
16 **a soft spot for little girls, especially ones dressed in red, so I ask**
17 **her, "Little girl, what's wrong?" She sobs that someone's out**
18 **to get her and someone can go choke on a poison apple for all**
19 **she cares. In this forest, those are pretty harsh words, so I ask**
20 **her, "Who's out to harm a sweet thing like you?" "My**
21 **granny," she says all weepy, those big brown eyes all red with**
22 **tears. Well, I get mushy and weak and forget to leave strange**
23 **little girls alone, so I ask if there's anything I could do to help.**
24   **She proceeds to tell me her life story, all ten years of it**
25 **anyway, about how her Granny treated her like a slave,**
26 **working her small fingers to the bone, how she froze during**
27 **the cold nights in the forest with only her red cape to keep her**
28 **warm, how Granny locked her up in a cage until she grew fat**
29 **so she could eat her. Truly horrible crimes. She said, "And now**
30 **she has a huntsman after my heart! I won't go back! Never!"**

1   Well, I'd never heard of such a thing. Sure, you hear
2   outrageous stories from these woods but usually from the
3   outsiders. For the most part, we're a peaceful community. I
4   was shocked.
5   "Is there anything I can do?" I asked again. I don't
6   know why I ever asked such a question. I was suckered in
7   by this red-caped delinquent. It wasn't until it was almost
8   too late that I learned how dangerous she could be.
9   She looks up and asks if I would go back with her to
10   Granny's house, to collect her things. I'd be a bodyguard,
11   me being a wolf and all. It sounded like the least I could do.
12   To make a long story short, when we got to her house,
13   she asks me to look inside to make sure Granny isn't
14   lurking in the corners waiting to strike. As soon as I was
15   inside, she starts screaming and shouting for her granny.
16   Granny jumps out from behind the door and bolts it shut.
17   A man dressed like the Queen's Own bursts out of the
18   wardrobe. "Shoot it! Shoot it!" Red yells. "I want a new
19   coat! Shoot it!" In desperation, I break one of the cottage
20   windows and escape. And now, I stand before you, out of
21   breath, on the run, hunted like a common wolf and all
22   because I have a soft spot for little girls, especially when
23   they're dressed in red.
24
25
26
27
28
29
30
31
32
33
34
35

Pea of Destiny

1   *(Court official walks On-stage cradling a tiny "book." Note:*
2 *Actor can "read" the excerpt from the pea's diary or actual "pea"*
3 *could read his own.)* **Your Honor, I'd like to submit the**
4 **following as evidence. This is the diary of the very same pea**
5 **that was selected by the prince to prove the princess'**
6 **worthiness. May I read an entry?** *(Pause)*
7   **June fifteenth. The sun was especially warm today. As it's**
8 **quite cramped in here, I shall have to be brief. I am green, I**
9 **am plump, and if the rumors are true, I feel I am destined for**
10 **greatness. How I can be so certain that I will not wind up in**
11 **someone's soup I can't say, but I feel bound for a larger**
12 **purpose than the dinner table.**
13   **June sixteenth. When my day started, I was sure that my**
14 **prediction was hopelessly false. About noon, our pod was**
15 **plucked by rough hands and plunked into a hard metal**
16 **container. Though I couldn't see where we were going, I could**
17 **feel our pod being lifted. The voices and questions of the others**
18 **around me were panicked and fearful, but I was trying to hold**
19 **onto hope. After a while, our pod was ruthlessly ripped apart**
20 **and we fell pea over pea into a washbasin. We were then**
21 **doused with a virtual waterfall and those rough hands stirred**
22 **and sifted the whole collection of us until I was separated from**
23 **my brothers and sisters. I landed nearest to the top of the**
24 **heap. From this position, I had a splendid view of the kitchen.**
25 **Moments later, a young man walked into the room and came**
26 **straight over to me. I could sense my luck changing. He**
27 **plucked me from the group (all I can think is that I was more**
28 **plump than most or perhaps, my position gave me a**
29 **prominence that I, from my point of view, was unaware.) He**
30 **tossed me once into the air, caught me and put me in his**

1   pocket. I rolled about quite happily enjoying my new
2   freedom. Up until that moment, I did not realize how
3   perfectly my shape was suited for rolling. When the young
4   man reached for me again, he curled me gently in his fist
5   and shoved me deep into the most comfortable darkness I
6   could imagine. In all my days in the pod, I was never so
7   comfortable. He left me and I could not help wonder what
8   would become of me. Then this heavy weight began
9   pressing down upon me. I tensed up with all my might and
10   became as hard and solid a pea as possible. I stayed that
11   way for I know not how long.
12   At long last, the weight was lifted and then the now
13   familiar hand reached in for me. When I emerged into the
14   light, there was applause and laughter and music and oh, I
15   felt as though my green skin would burst from happiness. I
16   had endured trials, I had been tested, and I had been found
17   worthy. I was truly a pea of destiny.
18
19
20
21
22
23
24
25
26
27
28
29
30
31
32
33
34
35

Princess V. Pea

1   (PRINCESS walks On-stage and sits Center Stage as if on
2 trial.) I swear to tell the truth, the whole truth and nothing but
3 the truth. (Pause) I am not really a princess. One morning, I
4 woke up and saw this story in the paper about a prince who
5 was running some sort of contest in order to find his future
6 bride. All you had to do was show up at the castle, spend the
7 night, and correctly identify the hidden object in the mattress
8 you'd been sleeping on. According to the paper, the prince
9 thought that only a real princess would be sensitive enough to
10 tell, which would get him the real thing for a wife.
11   I couldn't believe it. It seemed so easy. Go to sleep a
12 working class girl, wake up a princess. Now that was my kind
13 of deal. So, I went to the castle and knocked. I waited in line
14 with a group of girls, and after signing my name to about a
15 thousand forms, I was shown to a room. I've never seen a bed
16 so big. A coverlet on top of ten featherbeds on top of fifty
17 mattresses. I was nervous but I needed this princess gig badly.
18 My rent was due and I had a dollar-fifty in the bank. Besides,
19 compared to the other girls, I was a pro. If seven years at Big
20 Bernie's Mattress Barn hadn't prepared me to sleep in this
21 bed, nothing would. So, I climbed up this amazingly high
22 ladder and got into bed. I lay really still and tried to feel what
23 object was hidden underneath. I lay left. I lay right. I tossed
24 and turned. I even took off all my clothes and lay there naked
25 hoping that would help me figure out this hidden object. All I
26 could feel was down and fluff and satin sheets and darn it, if I
27 didn't get the best night's sleep I ever had. The next morning,
28 everyone filed down into the great hall to be served breakfast.
29 I thought it was weird to be served an omelet with peas in it.
30 Who serves peas with eggs? But I ate it just like everyone else.

1   After breakfast, the prince started quizzing everyone
2 about the hidden object. No one was getting it right and
3 Princey was getting more downhearted as if his plan wasn't
4 gonna work. When he asked me how did I sleep, all I could
5 think about was the peas in the omelet. So, I made up this
6 story about how I slept great except for this little spot that
7 kept stabbing me in the back. Princey looked so hopeful
8 that I nearly stopped there and told him the truth, but then
9 I remembered my rent. "I think it was a pea," I said.
10 Honestly, I just guessed. Well, these lights and sirens started
11 going off and balloons and confetti rained down from the
12 ceiling and the prince got down on one knee and proposed
13 right then and there. Your honor, princess or mattress
14 tester, I won fair and square, and it doesn't take royal
15 brains to figure that out.
16
17
18
19
20
21
22
23
24
25
26
27
28
29
30
31
32
33
34
35

One of His Loyal Subjects

1 *(Student walks On-stage shaking his head in disbelief.)* **Now**
2 I've seen everything. And boy, do I mean everything! I'm hot
3 too, but to strut through town as naked as a new baby? Why,
4 you've got to wonder if the man is all right in the head!
5   I had heard the rumor, but it was too ridiculous to believe,
6 even coming from the palace. You should know that our dear
7 king has a long history of nutty ideas. One time, he had his
8 royal inventors create a set of wings for him. No one knew
9 what he was going to do with them and by the time they
10 figured it out, our majesty had strapped them on and jumped
11 from the highest tower flapping madly. I didn't think the crazy
12 old fool would live to see another winter solstice but he did.
13   Then there was the time he tried breathing underwater.
14 Not like a fish, but through a hollow reed held above the
15 surface. I think the notion was that he could talk with the fish,
16 but as the king's luck would have it, an acorn dropped right
17 out of the tree and landed smack inside the reed while the king
18 was underwater. He sucked so hard for air that he sucked that
19 acorn straight into his windpipe.
20   So, the fact that the king thought he had enchanted fabric
21 wasn't surprising. Still, what if the fabric was enchanted?
22 What if the king really did have someone at the palace who
23 could do such a thing? I didn't want to be the only one in the
24 village who couldn't see the fabric, so I pretended to see it
25 right along with the rest of them.
26   I must admit, he looked cool. I, myself, was sweating like a
27 pig, such a hot day as it was. But there was our majesty, head
28 up, shoulders back, waving and smiling as if the day was as
29 pleasant as the first balmy day after the winter thaw.
30   Then this little tad of a fellow stepped out into the street.

1 All around me, people were murmuring about the exquisite
2 colors of the fabric or the artistic drape of the shawl.
3 Tommy looked from one adult to the other, and then at me.
4 I just shrugged my shoulders. He pointed at the king and
5 said loudly to the rest of us, "That man is naked!" Well,
6 everyone gasped and acted shocked and Tommy's mother
7 clapped her hand over his mouth as fast as she could. What
8 would the king say?

Now, here is your chance to write your own monolog. Pretend that you are the king from "The Emperor's New Clothes." What *do* you say? If you're at a loss for words, consider the monolog "In the Buff" as a possible response, but keep in mind there are only as many possibilities as lie in your imagination. Some things to consider when writing the king's monolog:

- What would make you walk naked through the streets?
- What events would lead up to that walk? What would happen after?
- How would you respond to your loyal subjects?
- What words would a king use to express himself?
- What kind of king do you want to be?

Remember, there's no right or wrong answer here. Just think kingly thoughts and break a leg!

In the Buff

1   (Student strolls onto the stage fanning himself. He may wear
2   an undershirt and brightly colored boxers. He should also project
3   an air of dignity.) **Is it hot enough for you?** (Waits for audience
4   response.) **Did you like my new clothes? I know what you're**
5   **thinking — the king has lost his marbles. He's a nut, a cuckoo,**
6   **a loony bird. My loyal subjects, let me put your minds at ease.**
7   **Your king is not crazy. Your king is just hot.**
8   **Perhaps, from your position in life, you think that the king**
9   **has it fairly easy. Good food, nice home, fancy clothes. True, I**
10   **do have these things, but being king is harder than it looks.**
11   **Everyone, each of you included, expects me to maintain a**
12   **royal image. Even in times of great stress, you expect me to**
13   **maintain my composure. Day after day, week after week, year**
14   **after year. I must admit, it gets to be a bit much. Especially**
15   **during a heat wave. So, I thought of a plan to unwind and let**
16   **you see that I'm not so different from you, and now, since I'm**
17   **finally cool, I'll be happy to share this plan with you.**
18   **Last week, my royal tailor came to visit to measure me for**
19   **a suit to wear during our summer festival. Now who in their**
20   **right mind wants to wear a suit in the summer heat? When he**
21   **asked me what type of suit I wanted to wear, I jokingly said,**
22   **"My birthday suit." At the time, it was just a joke, but I'll have**
23   **to admit that it did get me thinking. Why not wear my**
24   **birthday suit? In fact, what could be cooler? As the king, I**
25   **should be able to wear what I wanted. But my wife and tailor**
26   **would have nothing to do with it. They insisted that the king**
27   **should be decent, respectable, a model for his people. So, I did**
28   **what any king in this position would do: I sent my wife on**
29   **vacation and fired my tailor. Instead, I hired two gypsies to**
30   *pretend* **to be tailors. They would pretend to sew me a new**

1 summer suit for the festival. I must say, they were brilliant.
2 They made a big show out of pretending to sew and would
3 hold up invisible bolts of fabric for everyone to admire.
4 When anyone else would question what they were doing,
5 they said it was enchanted fabric and that only the truly
6 wise could see it. Well, no one in the castle wanted to be
7 thought of as unwise, so they all played along.
8   This morning, I put on my "new suit." It fit me like a
9 skin. *(Laughs at own wittiness.)* I'd never been so
10 comfortable since this horrible heat wave started. No hot
11 velvet breeches. No itchy neck ruffle, no suffocating ermine
12 cape. Just me as free as the breeze. It was well known to me
13 that the rumor about wisdom and my new suit had leaked
14 into the village. Not one of you said a word as I paraded
15 down the street. That is, until Tommy stepped out of the
16 crowd. Loud as you please, he called out in the fearless voice
17 of a child, "That man is naked!" How surprising that the
18 wisest person in our kingdom is a child. He saw me for who
19 I truly am — a man. A person's appearance is only part of
20 who they are. And just like you, my subjects, the real person
21 is not what you see, but who I am inside. And what I am is
22 hot.
23
24
25
26
27
28
29
30
31
32
33
34
35

About the Author

Heather Henderson caught the theater bug at an early age but never got to say a line on-stage until she was a senior in high school. She performed in many ballets (where you're not allowed to talk) and then, in her first high school production, was cast as a deaf/mute character! It was not until *West Side Story* that she was able to utter the very memorable line, "Ooh, oobley, ooh" as Riff's girlfriend, Velma.

After high school, Heather attended Florida State University (and again, she didn't get to say any lines in *The Merry Widow*) where she decided to become a teacher. Following graduation, Heather taught drama for four years at Galaxy Middle School in Deltona, Florida, teaching students to say all the lines she was never able to. She currently teaches seventh grade Language Arts at Heritage Middle School in Deltona.

Order Form

Meriwether Publishing Ltd.
PO Box 7710
Colorado Springs CO 80933-7710
Phone: 800-937-5297   Fax: 719-594-9916
Website: www.meriwetherpublishing.com

Please send me the following books:

_____ **The Flip Side II #BK-B247** $15.95
by Heather H. Henderson
60 more point-of-view monologs for teens

_____ **The Flip Side #BK-B221** $14.95
by Heather H. Henderson
64 point-of-view monologs for teens

_____ **Winning Monologs for Young Actors** $15.95
#BK-B127
by Peg Kehret
Honest-to-life monologs for young actors

_____ **Encore! More Winning Monologs for** $15.95
Young Actors #BK-B144
by Peg Kehret
More honest-to-life monologs for young actors

_____ **Acting Natural #BK-B133** $15.95
by Peg Kehret
Honest-to-life monologs, dialogs and playlets for teens

_____ **Teens Have Feelings, Too! #BK-B238** $14.95
by Deborah Karczewski
100 monologs for young performers

_____ **Theatre Games for Young Performers** $16.95
#BK-B188
by Maria C. Novelly
Improvisations and exercises for developing acting skills

**These and other fine Meriwether Publishing books are available at
your local bookstore or direct from the publisher. Prices subject to
change without notice. Check our website or call for current prices.**

Name: _____

Organization name: _____

Address: _____

City: _____ State: _____

Zip: _____ Phone: _____

❑ **Check enclosed**

❑ **Visa / MasterCard / Discover #** _____

Signature: _____   Expiration
date: _____
(required for credit card orders)

Colorado residents: Please add 3% sales tax.
Shipping: Include $2.75 for the first book and 50¢ for each additional book ordered.

❑ *Please send me a copy of your complete catalog of books and plays.*